The Psychobiology
of Human Motivation

WITHDRAWN
FROM STOCK

The Psychobiology of Human Motivation explores a core area of undergraduate psychology courses, the motivational processes that direct our behaviour, from basic physiological needs like hunger and thirst, sex and sleep to more complex aspects of social behaviour like altruism. Hugh Wagner explores the limits of biological explanations and shows how humans can influence 'basic' physiological drives in order to adapt to a complex social environment.

This textbook has four features that distinguish it from most other texts on physiological psychology or psychobiology. It is aimed at those taking modules in human motivation, concentrating on the biological bases specifically of motivation. Second, the physiological and anatomical content has been carefully tailored to the needs of the issues discussed. Third, it explores the limitations of the attempt to explain human motivation in terms of animal physiological models and, fourth, it considers cognitive and social motivation from a psychobiological perspective. This concise and useful text will be welcomed by students of psychology, health and education at all levels.

Hugh Wagner is Senior Lecturer in the Department of Psychology at the University of Manchester. He has taught psychobiology courses for 22 years and published numerous chapters and journal articles on emotion and eating disorders. He is the author, with P. Lloyd and others, of *Introduction to Psychology* (1984).

Psychology Focus

Series editor: Perry Hinton, Oxford Brookes University

The Psychology Focus series provides students with a new focus on key topic areas in psychology. It supports students taking modules in psychology, whether for a psychology degree or a combined programme, and those renewing their qualification in a related discipline. Each short book:

■ presents clear, in-depth coverage of a discrete area with many applied examples
■ assumes no prior knowledge of psychology
■ has been written by an experienced teacher
■ has chapter summaries, annotated further reading and a glossary of key terms.

Also available in this series:

Friendship in Childhood and Adolescence
Phil Erwin

Gender and Social Psychology
Viv Burr

Jobs, Technology and People
Nik Chmiel

Learning and Studying
James Hartley

Personality: A Cognitive Approach
Jo Brunas-Wagstaff

Intelligence and Abilities
Colin Cooper

Stress, Cognition and Health
Tony Cassidy

The Social Psychology of Behaviour in Small Groups
Donald C. Pennington

Types of Thinking
Ian Robertson

Psychobiology of Human Motivation
Hugh Wagner

Stereotypes, Cognition and Culture
Perry R. Hinton

Psychology and 'Human Nature'
Peter Ashworth

Abnormal Psychology
Alan Carr

Attitudes and Persuasion
Phil Erwin

The Person in Social Psychology
Viv Burr

Introducing Neuropsychology
John Stirling

The Psychobiology of Human Motivation

■ Hugh Wagner

Psychology Press
Taylor & Francis Group

HOVE AND NEW YORK

First published 1999
by Routledge
11 New Fetter Lane, London
EC4P 4EE

Simultaneously published in
the USA and Canada
by Routledge
29 West 35th Street, New York
NY 10001

© 1999 Hugh Wagner

Reprinted 2004 and 2008
by Psychology Press
27 Church Road, Hove, East Sussex
BN3 2FA
270 Madison Avenue, New York
NY 10016

Transferred to Digital Printing 2011

Typeset in Sabon and Futura by
Florence Production Ltd, Stoodleigh,
Devon

This publication has been produced
with paper manufactured to strict
environmental standards and with pulp
derived from sustainable forests.

*British Library Cataloguing in
Publication Data*
A catalogue record for this book is
available from the British Library

*Library of Congress Cataloging in
Publication Data*
Wagner, Hugh L.
  The psychobiology of human
  motivation / Hugh Wagner.
    (Psychology focus)
  Includes bibliographical references.
  1. Motivation (Psychology)
  2. Psychobiology. I. Title.
  II. Series.
BF503.W34   1999
153.8–dc21   98–41034

ISBN 978-0-415-19275-0 (pbk)

For Rachel, Jessica, and Emma

Contents

CONTENTS

Illustrations

Figures

Tables

Series preface

The Psychology Focus series provides short, up-to-date accounts of key areas in psychology without assuming the reader's prior knowledge in the subject. Psychology is often a favoured subject area for study, since it is relevant to a wide range of disciplines such as Sociology, Education, Nursing and Business Studies. These relatively inexpensive but focused short texts combine sufficient detail for psychology specialists with sufficient clarity for non-specialists.

The series authors are academics experienced in undergraduate teaching as well as research. Each takes a key topic within their area of psychological expertise and presents a short review, highlighting important themes and including both theory and research findings. Each aspect of the topic is clearly explained with supporting glossaries to elucidate technical terms.

The series has been conceived within the context of the increasing modularisation which has been developed in higher education over the last decade and fulfils the consequent need for clear, focused, topic-based course material. Instead of following one course of study, students on a modularisation programme are often able to choose modules from a wide range of disciplines to complement the modules they are required to study for a specific degree. It can no longer be assumed that students studying a particular module will necessarily have the same background knowledge (or lack of it!) in that subject. But they will need to familiarise themselves with a particular topic since a single module in a single topic may be only 15 weeks long, with assessments arising during that period. They may have to combine eight or more modules in a single year to obtain a degree at the end of their programme of study.

One possible problem with studying a range of separate modules is that the relevance of a particular topic or the relationship between topics may not always be apparent. In the Psychology Focus series authors have drawn where possible on practical and applied examples to support the points being made so that readers can see the wider relevance of the topic under study. Also, the study of psychology is usually broken up into separate areas, such as social psychology, developmental psychology and cognitive psychology, to take three examples. Whilst the books in the Psychology Focus series will provide excellent coverage of certain key topics within these 'traditional' areas, the authors have not been constrained in their examples and explanations and may draw on material across the whole field of psychology to help explain the topic under study more fully.

Each text in the series provides the reader with a range of important material on a specific topic. They are suitably comprehensive and give a clear account of the important issues involved. The authors analyse and interpret the material as well as present an up-to-date and detailed review of key work. Recent references are provided along with suggested further reading to allow readers to investigate the topic in more depth. It is hoped, therefore, that after following the informative review of a key topic in a Psychology Focus text, readers will not only have a clear understanding of the issues in question but will be intrigued and challenged to investigate the topic further.

Acknowledgements

I thank Kate Wagner for guidance with genetics and molecular biology, Stephanie van Goozen for generously sharing her work on human aggression and sexuality, and Martin Lea for help with the production of the figures. I am also grateful to my students over the past few years for their generous feedback on my teaching of the course from which this book is derived.

The author and publishers would like to thank all the copyright holders of material reproduced in this volume for granting permission to include it. Every effort was made to contact authors and copyright holders. If proper acknowledgement has not been made, the copyright holders should contact the publishers.

Chapter 1

Introduction and overview

Motivation

Psychologists and non-psychologists alike have always wanted to explain *why* people do the things that they do. Different people seem to be driven by different motives: while one devotes the majority of his or her time to achieving the largest possible business empire, another chooses to focus on creating beautiful works of art. While one strives to achieve the greatest possible success in a chosen field, another just wants a quiet and relatively anonymous life. Such considerations give rise to many questions about the nature of motivation. Are we all driven by the same basic motives so that business success and artistic creativity equally satisfy the same underlying need? Or are they qualitatively different types of motivation? How are different motives related to one another? Are some motives basic and others in some way secondary to, or derived from them? How does the satisfaction of one motive affect other motivation? Are there specifically human types of motivation, or are human motives elaborations of motives that we share with other species? To what extent are we aware of the motives that govern our own behaviour?

All behaviour except the simplest reflexes is considered to be motivated. Motivation controls behaviour and is usually regarded as having two aspects: it *energises* behaviour and *directs* it towards some goal. Motives can be classified in numerous ways as can attempts to explain them. Bearing in mind that it is impossible to separate completely classifications and explanations, in this section we will look briefly at general issues concerning types of motivation and theories of motivation.

Types of motivation

Maslow (1954) proposed that human motivation has a hierarchical structure which he called a *hierarchy of needs* (see Table 1.1). This hierarchy provides a useful starting point for our overview of motivation, and although I will not pursue Maslow's theory beyond this, I will take issue with some details. At the

TABLE 1.1 Maslow's hierarchy of needs and an alternative classification

Maslow's hierarchy		Alternative view	
Level of need	*Motivation*	*Motivation*	*Type of motive*
Self-actualisation	curiosity	cognitive consistency	Cognitive motives
	peak experiences creative living fulfilling work		
Esteem	confidence	achievement	Self-integrative motives
	mastery self-respect	self-esteem	
Love	free expression	self-presentation	Social motives
	sense of warmth sense of growing together	cooperation altruism	
Safety	security	aggression	Non-homeostatic
	comfort calm	sex ?curiosity	
Physiological	fatigue sex hunger thirst	?sleep hunger thirst	Homeostatic

lowest level in Maslow's hierarchy are *physiological needs*. These are needs which appear to have a basis in physiological changes. We have to make a further distinction amongst physiological needs which derive from imbalances in the body, like hunger and thirst, which we will call *homeostatic needs*, and those which do not have the function of maintaining bodily equilibrium, which we will call *non-homeostatic needs*. The homeostatic needs that I focus on in this book are the needs for sleep ('fatigue'), thirst and hunger. In Chapters 3, 4 and 5 I examine the physiological mechanisms of each of these and also consider their biological importance and psychological influences on them.

In Maslow's hierarchy, non-homeostatic needs are represented by sex, and we will look at the origins of sexual behaviour, and some of its variations, in Chapter 6. Another non-homeostatic need that we will look at is aggression. Although this is absent from Maslow's hierarchy it could perhaps belong with the next level of needs, needs for *safety*, since it is partly concerned with defence of the animal. However, it also serves reproductive functions and so might be considered with the physiological needs. We look at these functions of aggression, their origins and control in Chapter 7.

The first two levels in the hierarchy are together described as *basic needs*. This term is something of a problem as its use is not consistent from writer to writer. These needs are basic in Maslow's hierarchy because they are at the bottom of the pile and must be satisfied before other needs can be attended to. (This, by the way, is one problem with Maslow's approach, since it does not allow, for example, for the phenomenon of the artist starving in a garret: out of adversity comes creativity.) But 'basic' can also mean *fundamental*, in the sense that other motives are derived from them.

The next two levels of need in the hierarchy are together described as *psychological needs*. The lower of these is called 'love' but is actually composed of a variety of *social motives* based on group membership. Next are needs that Maslow called 'esteem', which we shall include as *self-integration motives*. We will examine these cognitive and social motives briefly in Chapter 9. Finally come *self-actualisation needs*. While these include curiosity and the avoidance of boredom (which we will look at with cognitive motivation in Chapter 9), they are presented by Maslow as the summit of human motivation. People operating at this motivational level, 'self-actualisers', are considered to be on a higher personal level. The hierarchy can be viewed as representing the sequence in which needs arose during evolution and may relate to mechanisms in parts of the brain that evolved at different stages. This is another way in which those lower in the hierarchy might be called 'basic'.

Approaches to motivation

My earlier general comments about motivation mixed terms suggesting a mechanistic approach (e.g. 'driven') with terms suggesting self-direction (e.g. 'chooses'). Most approaches to motivation have tended towards the mechanistic. Quite early in the history of psychology the dominant view was that human and animal motivation was determined by a number of instincts. The dominant instinct theorist within mainstream psychology was McDougall (1908), who defined an instinct as 'an inherited or innate psychological disposition to perceive, and pay attention to, objects of a certain class ... and to act in regard to [them] in a particular manner, or, at least, to experience an impulse to such action'. The second part of this definition clearly describes motivation. McDougall recognised eighteen instincts, mostly corresponding to the three lowest levels of Maslow's hierarchy of needs. Thus, motives are innately determined, although McDougall argued that they could be modified by experience, and that we can control whether or not we act on our impulses.

At about the same time the other major instinct theorist, Freud, was developing his view that all motivation was ultimately reducible to two basic and opposed sources of energy, the life instinct and the death instinct (see Freud, 1922). Freud insisted that we are not generally aware of the operation of these instincts, which are unconscious sources of motivation. Further, all acts, including apparently unmotivated acts like slips of the tongue, are in fact motivated, revealing to the initiated some aspect of our unconscious motivation. Our usual explanations for our behaviour do not relate to our true unconscious motives.

More recent approaches have continued the generally mechanistic approach of these early theorists. The homeostatic motives are commonly viewed from a physiological perspective. That is, they serve clearly defined bodily needs and the approach is to identify the physiological mechanisms through which the needs are assessed and their satisfaction achieved. We will look at the principles of this approach in Chapter 4. Generally the approach is to consider that a need arises from a specific tissue deficit. This leads to a **drive** that energises (and perhaps directs) the animal to consummatory behaviour that satisfies the need. There is little useful debate about the general nature of this motivational system, apart from difference of opinion about whether drive states are specific to particular needs or whether they operate as a general state. But this book is not a physiology text and we will want to go beyond the description of physiological mechanisms. The aim of the approach taken by this book is *to explore the limits of physiological explanation of human motivation.* In each chapter we will look at the ways in which humans can control or otherwise influence the 'basic' physiological drives.

Drive-reduction theories attempt to explain non-physiological motivation in a way that is parallel to physiological motivation. That is, people are assumed to pass into a state of deprivation akin to the tissue deficit of a homeostatic need. This leads to a drive state that is either general, or specific to the particular state of deprivation. This drive leads the person into 'consummatory' behaviour that relieves the state of deprivation. As a simple example, which we will look at more closely in Chapter 9, deprivation of novel stimulation leads to a state which we experience as boredom and which reflects a drive to seek out stimulation. When novel stimulation is found the deprivation is reduced and boredom disappears.

Drive-reduction theories date mostly from the **behaviourist** period in psychology, and were actually applied not to psychological needs but to physiological needs as the basis of theories of learning. Because the reduction of a drive is pleasant it rewards behaviour that immediately precedes it, that is it makes that behaviour more likely to occur. Learning theorists such as Hull

(1943) described drive as non-specific, that is capable of energising any behaviour and supporting any kind of learning. Further consideration of learning theory is beyond the scope of this book. We will return to the issue of specificity or generality of drive in Chapter 9.

Learning theorists described the physiological drives as primary drives in the sense that the drives arise internally but are directed by external stimuli. Learning can modify the external stimuli with which the drive is associated. The theorists attempted to apply these principles to other types of motivation which they described as *secondary drives*. These were learned in the sense that the source of the motivation is learned but the drive state itself is the same as for a primary drive. When an initially neutral stimulus is paired with the satisfaction of a primary drive, that stimulus itself comes to evoke a similar drive state. This was said to be demonstrated by conditioned emotional responses. Pairing of a frightening stimulus (an electric shock or a loud noise) with a previously neutral stimulus led to the neutral stimulus itself becoming frightening. However, it was impossible to demonstrate empirically this sort of process taking place for the 'higher' motives of human beings, and it seems intrinsically far-fetched to explain a thirst for knowledge, glory, pride, creativity and so on as conditioned responses.

Modern approaches to motivation borrow the language of drive-reduction theory, but apply it in a more general way. Thus, the term 'drive' does not have the implications of Hullian learning theory but is used to describe the state of feeling motivated to perform some action. A 'need' does not relate to a tissue deficit but to an experienced (usually) feeling that something is missing. Much of the analysis of psychological motivation derives from social psychology as we will see in Chapter 9. However, under-lying all of these approaches is the view that the satisfaction of needs or drives is pleasant. In Chapter 8 we will look at brain mechanisms that are thought to underlie the effects of reward, reinforcement and pleasure. We look at these mechanisms in the context of addiction, which, it has been argued, is based on the stimulation of these brain centres.

The biological bases of behaviour

Everyday language makes use of numerous analogies between people and animals. Many of these refer to people's behaviour or motivation. For example, gluttonous people eat 'like pigs', somebody who acts dishonourably is a 'rat' and more generally we refer to people who do not control themselves in acceptable ways as behaving 'like animals'. Many of these analogies are pejorative: they imply that human behaviour and motivation are superior to those of animals. At the same time, however, the use of such phrases clearly recognises that the comparison of humans with other species is useful at some level. Their use also suggests that there are common features to human and animal motivation, and that humans are distinguished by our ability to surmount these common features. This book seeks to explore the extent to which we and other animals share common features of motivation, and to identify ways in which human motivation has to be considered unique. To put this another way, I will be examining the biological bases of human motivation.

There are many ways in which biology can inform our study of psychology. In one sense our understanding of human behaviour is enhanced by considering our 'animal' nature. Later in this section I will be more specific about the different ways that the biological bases of behaviour can be explored. Each of these ways depends on recognising the place that human beings, members of the species *Homo sapiens*, occupy in the animal kingdom, and what this implies about continuity between species and differences between species. The underlying principle on which examining the biological bases of human behaviour rests is the fact of evolution.

Evolution and genetics

The concept of evolution is inextricably linked to the name of Charles Darwin, following the publication in 1859 of his book *The Origin of Species*. However, for at least 100 years before that, biologists had speculated about the possibility that modern species are derived from earlier ones. What Darwin did was to suggest a mechanism for evolution, namely that it proceeded by a process of **natural selection**: the 'survival of the fittest'.

One of the main tasks naturalists set themselves in the eighteenth century and later was the classification of animals (and plants) into groups of like species, a process called taxonomy. Until very recently taxonomy was based almost entirely on similarities of structural features of species. Species were placed into a 'tree' of species related to one another in different degrees by these similarities. The concept of evolution made sense of these relationships amongst species, known now as the **phylogenetic tree**. More similar animals are so because they have diverged from a common ancestor more recently in evolutionary history than less similar ones. Now that techniques of molecular biology are being applied to the question of taxonomy, the results have largely confirmed the original classification based on structure.

All of the tissues and chemical constituents of our bodies derive from **genes** which we inherit from our parents. Each gene carries the code for the production of a particular protein or other molecule. These molecules (either directly or indirectly) form the basis of cell and tissue development. Each gene is part of a very large molecule called **deoxyribonucleic acid** (or **DNA**). Each DNA molecule is looped and bound to a central matrix to form a **chromosome**. Human beings have 23 pairs of chromosomes and inherit one half of each pair from each parent. The genetic make-up of the individual organism is called its **genotype**. The extent to which a gene exerts its effect depends on environmental influences, and the resulting physical (and by extension psychological) features of the individual are known as the **phenotype**. This is true, for example, of genes that specify physical characteristics like height; inheriting genes for tall stature will only ensure that you are tall if you are adequately nourished during growth. When we look at genetic influences on behaviour in this book we will invariably find that such genetic determinants are not only highly dependent on environmental factors, but also that genetic influences on behaviour are **polygenic**, meaning that two or more genes help to establish variations in a particular behaviour or characteristic.

There are many ways of trying to establish the extent to which some behaviour is determined by genetic factors. In humans, most studies look at how similar people of different degrees of family relationship are. Monozygotic (identical) twins who have an identical genotype should be most similar. Dizygotic (fraternal) twins have 50 per cent of their genes in common, just as do any other siblings, and the proportion of shared genes decreases as relationships become more distant. Unfortunately, of course, similarities of environmental influence vary in a parallel manner, making it difficult to disentangle the two influences. The best studies of this type have compared monozygotic twins reared together with those reared apart following adoption. In other species selective breeding produces strains that vary in behavioural characteristics, demonstrating a genetic basis for those characteristics. Ultimately the aim of behavioural genetics is to identify actual genes and their locations that affect psychological characteristics.

The techniques of molecular biology are based on transferring fragments of DNA to simple organisms (usually bacteria or yeasts) to produce recombinant DNA. The fast replication of the bacteria permits the extraction of large numbers of clones (identical copies) of the original DNA. DNA cloning permits the identification of the genetic make-up of a particular organism, and of the sites and nature of the genes which code for particular molecules, and hence control the development of particular structures and functions. The implications of this technology are enormous, since not only can genes be identified, but they can be transferred to other species, and can be passed on to the offspring of such transgenic animals. This permits a variety of medical and commercial applications.

In the present context these techniques have two significant applications. First, they permit the location of behaviourally significant genes. Second, they allow biologists to define phylogenetic relationships in terms of the similarity of the DNA of different species. For example, our closest relatives are chimpanzees; we share more than 98 per cent of the DNA of chimpanzees and slightly less than 98 per cent of that of gorillas. This may seem startling; are we really so similar to these apes? But they are very misleading figures. First, most DNA actually has no known function for the individual organism. Second, most of the DNA that *does* code for proteins or other molecules, does so for molecules which form the basis of structure and function at the cellular level, and so it would be very surprising if it were different in different primate species. Clearly, while the common inheritance of DNA does establish phylogenetic continuity, it is necessary to bear in mind the importance of the 1.6 per cent or so of our DNA which we *do not* share with other species.

The feature that most clearly distinguishes the evolutionary line that leads to *Homo sapiens* is progressively larger brain size. In particular, this has involved an absolute and relative increase in the size of the **cerebral hemispheres** over 'lower' brain regions. We will look at this in more detail in the next chapter. The lower, phylogenetically older, parts of the brain are, as we shall see, of crucial importance in controlling basic bodily functions, and in motivation. The cerebral hemispheres provide for enhanced individual adaptability, and this increases as we go up the phylogenetic scale, culminating in the human brain. It is this individual adaptability that limits the extent to which the motivation of humans can be explained by underlying physiological mechanisms. But, while *Homo sapiens* has an enormous **cerebral cortex**, most of the structures of the older parts of the brain can still be identified, and are still of vital importance for human survival. We shall be looking particularly at these in this book.

Two final points about evolution need to be made clear before we proceed. First, the principle of natural selection applies at the level of the individual not of the group. That is, it is not the fittest *species* that survives but the fittest *individual*. Ultimately, enhanced individual fitness can lead to the establishment of a new species. Second, all present-day species are equally 'evolved' in the sense that they are all the current final step in their line of descent. In particular, we are *not* descended from any other existing species. Our line of descent diverged from that of the chimpanzees at a common ancestor some 5 to 7 million years ago.

Biological psychology

The terms biological psychology and psychobiology are general terms which include any approach to the subject matter of psychology that tries to place it into its biological context; that is, to examine the biological bases of behaviour. In its broadest sense this can be the examination of the evolution of human behaviour, a field known as evolutionary psychology. Principles from studies of the adaptive functions of structures and behaviours in other species are extended to try to explain human behaviour. Within animal biology in particular, the approach to social behaviour that this leads to is known as **sociobiology**. This is an approach that applies Darwinian principles to the study of social, and particularly reproductive, behaviour (see Dawkins, 1976). Here, in the notion of the **selfish gene**, the individual nature of natural selection is most clearly expressed. In this view all animal behaviour can be interpreted as having the goal of increasing the proportion of the individual's genes in the next generation.

Also directly related to evolutionary principles is the field of comparative psychology. Broadly this compares the behaviour of different species. Most frequently the species that are compared with humans are selected for convenience, and the process studied most often has been learning. Thus, much of what is called comparative psychology is about learning in rats. Usually it is assumed that the processes examined in other species are the same as those taking place in humans. In this book we will be concerned mainly with physiological psychology; the study of the physiological mechanisms underlying behaviour and mental processes. Since most of our information about physiological mechanisms of motivation comes from studies of laboratory animals (again, usually rats), the assumption of similarity of behaviour and underlying mechanism underlies most of the subject matter of this book.

It is impossible to understand the physiological mechanisms involved in motivation and emotion without some basic understanding of physiology. Chapter 2 is devoted to a brief account of the essentials of physiology for this purpose.

Summary

Most behaviour is considered to be motivated. Approaches to the understanding of motivation have varied enormously. It is useful to separate physiological needs from psychological motives. Homeostatic physiological needs like thirst and hunger clearly serve to satisfy deficits in the body, whereas other needs are less clearly homeostatic (sleep) or are non-homeostatic (sex and aggression). The main approach to these motives is to search for physiological mechanisms. Attempts to explain psychological motives have often been modelled on dominant views about physiological motives: that is, motivation consists of drives arising from needs that lead to behaviour directed at satisfying the needs.

Human beings have evolved from ancestors that we share with our closest 'relatives', the chimpanzees. The structure of our bodies is derived from genes on chromosomes which we inherit equally from each of our parents. The effect of each gene is dependent on environmental factors for its expression, and non-genetic influences are particularly important for genes that affect behavioural characteristics. The evolutionary line that leads to humans is characterised by the development of a large brain, particularly the cerebral hemispheres, which confer evolutionary advantages of increased adaptability and decreased reliance on more primitive and automatic brain structures. Psychobiology encompasses any approach to psychology that considers its biological context. This includes evolutionary psychology and sociobiology, which examine the evolutionary background to human behaviour; comparative psychology, which compares human and other species; and physiological psychology, which considers the physiological mechanisms of human psychology. We will be concerned mostly with the last of these.

Further reading

Lieberman, D. A. (1990) *Learning: Behavior and Cognition*, Belmont, CA: Wadsworth. This book gives a thorough grounding in learning theory and the view of motivation that it encompasses.

Plomin, R., DeFries, J. C., McClearn, G. E. and Rutter, M. (1997) *Behavioral Genetics*, third edition, New York: W. H. Freeman. The latest edition of this widely recommended text gives an introduction to the principles of genetics and to evolutionary psychology, but concentrates on describing what is known about the interaction of environmental and genetic factors in a variety of psychological areas.

Ridley, Mark (1996) *Evolution*, second edition, Cambridge, MA: Blackwell. A comprehensive, standard text on all aspects of evolution, from the molecular level to the emergence of human beings.

Segal, N. L., Weisfeld, G. E. and Weisfeld, C. C. (1997) *Uniting Psychology and Biology: Integrative Perspectives on Human Development*, Washington, DC: American Psychological Association. This recent volume brings together contributions from leading researchers, exploring the interrelationships of biological bases and socio-cultural influences in many of the topics touched on in the present book.

Chapter 2

Essentials of human physiology

MOTIVATION HAS ITS BASIS in physiological processes. In this chapter we will look at the anatomical structures underlying these mechanisms and the principles of physiology on which they operate. I will concentrate on the two major systems which organise the functions of the body: the nervous system and the endocrine system. I will only give sufficient detail for you to understand the location and function of components of those systems to which I refer in the remaining chapters.

The nervous system and the endocrine system frequently have similar effects on the body. One distinction between their effects is that the actions of the nervous system generally commence quickly and terminate quickly. In contrast, endocrine actions tend to take longer to start and last for longer. We will also see that the two systems are highly interrelated.

The nervous system

The nervous system is conveniently divided in two different ways. The first is a distinction between the **peripheral nervous system** and the **central nervous system (CNS)**. Cutting across this division is the distinction between the **autonomic nervous system (ANS)** and the **somatic nervous system**. The ANS and the somatic nervous system have both central and peripheral components. In this section, we will look at the major components and principles of action of these divisions.

The peripheral nervous system

The peripheral somatic nervous system consists of nerves which connect the sensory systems and the effector organs (e.g. muscles) to the CNS. Each nerve is a bundle of **axons** (fibres) which are extensions of the **neurones** or nerve cells (see Figure 2.1). Nerves carry commands away from the CNS to the various organs (**efferent** signals), and information back to the CNS from sensory systems (**afferent** signals), both from specialised organs like the eyes and ears, and from sensory receptors in the skin, muscles, joints and so on. The major functions of the peripheral somatic nervous system, then, are sensory and motor. It passes to the CNS information about the external environment and the individual's movement and position, and passes commands to the muscles to contract. The motor functions that the somatic nervous system controls are mostly under voluntary control. The exceptions are spinal reflexes, like the knee-jerk and those which co-ordinate the opposed contraction and relaxation of muscles in an action such as walking.

Signals do not travel along axons by simple electrical conduction, as in a wire, but are propagated by **depolarisation**, the active transport of ions of sodium and potassium across the **cell membrane**, the outer covering of the axon. This nerve impulse is known as the **action potential** of the neurone, and has an all-or-none nature. That is, it always has the same size regardless of the strength of any stimulus, provided that that stimulus reaches a

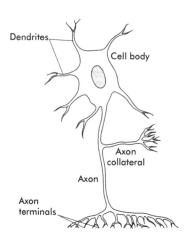

FIGURE 2.1 Diagrammatic representation of a typical neurone (*from A. Vander et al., 1994, Human Physiology, 6th edn, McGraw-Hill Companies, by permission*)

threshold, a minimum intensity required to produce sufficient depolarisation to initiate the action potential. Most 'connections' between neurones are again not like electrical connections, but are made by way of chemical transmission across a gap called a **synapse**. Synaptic transmission provides both greater flexibility and greater specificity than would simple electrical connections. We will look at how this works and its importance on pp. 23–5.

The central nervous system

The central nervous system comprises the *brain* and the *spinal cord*, each of which is composed of neurones and various other tissues. Most of the control and organising functions of the CNS are carried out by neurones. We will have little to say about the spinal cord, which mainly serves to channel sensory information to the brain and motor commands from the brain. We will concentrate here on the brain itself. The main brain regions to which we shall refer in this book, and some of their functions, are listed in Figure 2.2, and their locations are shown in Figure 2.3.

The brain is usefully subdivided on the basis of its development. In the embryo the brain first develops three distinct swellings known as the **forebrain**, the **midbrain**, and the **hindbrain**. Later in development the forebrain becomes divided into what will become the cerebral hemispheres and a region that will develop into the **thalamus** and **hypothalamus**. The cerebral hemispheres are further elaborated into, amongst others, the **neocortex**, which is the site of awareness of sensory input, of voluntary action and of symbolic activity like language; the **amygdala**, which is involved in motivational sensory processing; and the **corpus callosum**, a fibre bundle that joins corresponding parts of the left and right neocortex. The thalamus is a relay station in most of the sensory pathways into the brain. The hypothalamus will figure largely in later chapters as it is vitally important in the control of motivated behaviour. It also co-ordinates ANS activity (see pp. 21–2) and controls the **pituitary gland** (see p. 28).

The midbrain contains, amongst other structures, part of a network of neurones called the **reticular formation** which is

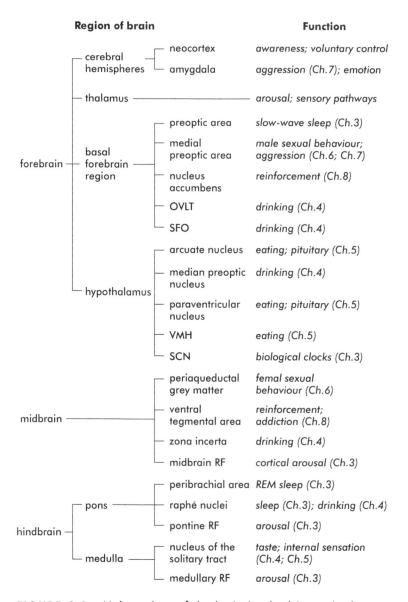

FIGURE 2.2 Main regions of the brain involved in motivation

important in maintaining the arousal of the CNS. In addition, there are a number of nuclei and fibre tracts concerned with various motivated behaviours, which we will return to in subsequent chapters.

The hindbrain develops into the cerebellum (which is concerned with motor co-ordination and some learning), the **pons** (which contains nuclei controlling movement, as well as sensory inputs from some cranial nerves), and the **medulla**. The medulla is the hindmost part of the brain and connects it to the spinal cord, hence fibres from the rest of the brain pass through it on their way to and from the spinal cord. The reticular formation extends from the midbrain into the medulla. The term **brain stem** is often applied to all of the midbrain and hindbrain structures apart from the cerebellum.

Centrally located throughout the CNS is a fluid-filled arrangement of canals and chambers. The chambers are known as the **cerebral ventricles**. This system is filled with a liquid, very similar in composition to the plasma of the blood, called **cerebrospinal fluid** (**CSF**). This arrangement has two functions. First, it provides a protective cushion against damage to the brain during movement. Second, since the CSF is in intimate contact with some

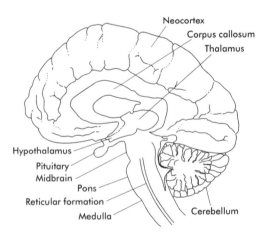

FIGURE 2.3 Diagrammatic section through the brain showing the main structures (after W.B. Webb, 1978, MacMillan Inc.)

important brain structures, as we shall see below, it provides a way in which some hormones act on brain centres.

The **capillaries** that supply blood to most areas of the brain are much less permeable than those in other parts of the body. This has led to the notion of a **blood–brain barrier**. There is a continuum of ease with which substances will cross the blood–brain barrier. Oxygen, carbon dioxide and water cross readily, glucose quite easily, ions like sodium and potassium more slowly, and many hormones and proteins cross to a very limited degree. The blood–brain barrier protects the brain from the effects of circulating substances that have effects on peripheral organs. The brain is essentially a neural mechanism with chemical transmission of information across synapses. If the chemical environment of the brain were not kept constant then widespread disruption of its activities would result.

Two other facts about the blood–brain barrier are important for our purposes. First, while some important, physiologically active substances effectively do not cross the barrier, closely related substances may do so. This means that the chemical **precursors** of some active substances can pass into the brain and affect its action after being converted into the active substance. Second, a group of brain centres in and around the hypothalamus, collectively known as the **circumventricular organs** (since they surround the third ventricle), does permit the passage of other substances, and is considered to be outside the blood–brain barrier. These organs serve as a route by which hormones secreted in the hypothalamus can pass into the blood stream. Conversely, they can themselves be affected by circulating hormones as we shall see in Chapter 4 in relation to thirst. They also probably release hormones into the CSF, from which they can affect other circumventricular organs.

The autonomic nervous system

The ANS co-ordinates the control of the internal environment (see Chapter 3), and those bodily functions that are basic for survival. It has both afferent and efferent components, and operates involuntarily and largely without our awareness. The central components of the ANS are in the hypothalamus, the brain stem and the spinal cord. The peripheral ANS is divided functionally into the **sympathetic nervous system** (SNS) and the **parasympathetic nervous system** (PNS). Most of our organ systems are innervated (supplied) by both branches, and the two act in a generally antagonistic manner, so that, for example, the state of constriction or dilatation of blood vessels is controlled by a dynamic equilibrium of inputs from the SNS and the PNS. This allows the resources of the body to be matched to its varying needs. For example, SNS activity increases the heart rate and decreases the activity of the digestive system, while PNS activity decreases the heart rate and promotes digestive activity. SNS activity tends to prepare the body to respond to emergency situations while PNS activity maintains the resting state of the body.

The afferent fibres of the ANS pass information about the state of the organs back to the CNS. There, they initiate corrective responses involving either the spinal cord alone or the hypothalamus. Hypothalamic responses to SNS afferents are generally co-ordinated responses over a number of organ systems, whereas spinal responses tend to be single organ responses. Pain information from internal organs is not represented separately from muscle and skin pain in the cerebral cortex. Visceral pain fibres synapse with somatic pain fibres that enter the spinal cord at the same place. For example, pain fibres from the heart enter the spinal cord with those from the upper left arm and chest and damage to the heart is experienced as pain in the upper left arm and chest. This is called referred pain.

Almost all ANS efferent fibres have a synapse between leaving the spinal cord and reaching the effector organs. SNS fibres leave the spinal cord at the dorsal and lumbar levels and pass to **ganglia** close to the spinal cord. For this reason the ANS fibres leaving the spinal cord are known as **preganglionic fibres**. After synapses in the ganglia the **postganglionic fibres** pass directly to the effector organs. Preganglionic fibres of the PNS leave the brain stem and the sacral region of the spinal cord and pass directly to synapses near the target organs. As we shall see in the next section, the actions of the SNS and PNS on the target cells depend on the secretion of different chemical messengers by the postganglionic neurones.

Synapses and neurotransmitters

As I pointed out on p. 18, most transmission of information between neurones takes place across synapses, by means of chemical substances secreted by one neurone and attaching to receptors on the next. In these chemical synapses, the axon terminals of the presynaptic neurone form **terminal buttons,** which are separated from the postsynaptic neurone by a narrow **synaptic cleft** (see Figure 2.4). Each postsynaptic neurone receives many terminal buttons and these can come from many different presynaptic neurones. The presynaptic neurone contains **synaptic vesicles** which contain a chemical known as a **neurotransmitter.** When an action potential reaches the synapse, it causes the vesicles to attach to the cell membrane and release the neurotransmitter into the cleft. The neurotransmitter attaches to **receptor molecules** in the membrane of the postsynaptic neurone. This attachment is specific since the neurotransmitter has exactly the right shape to fit the receptor molecule (a 'lock-and-key' mechanism). Once a

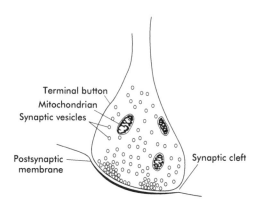

FIGURE 2.4 Simplified diagram of a chemical synapse (after C.R. Noback, 1967, The Human Nervous System, McGraw-Hill, by permission of the author)

23

transmitter is attached to a receptor it changes the **polarisation** of the neurone. If the effect of the transmitter is to depolarise the postsynaptic neurone it will increase its probability of firing. This is known as an excitatory effect. Conversely, the neurotransmitter might hyperpolarise the postsynaptic cell making it less likely to fire, an inhibitory effect. Whether the postsynaptic cell fires or not depends on the balance of excitatory and inhibitory influences. If enough excitatory receptors are stimulated, the depolarisation will be enough to start an action potential travelling along the postsynaptic neurone.

At the beginning of this chapter I pointed out that the actions of the nervous system are fast to start and fast to terminate. The fast start is the result of rapid electrical transmission through neurones, resulting in the release of neurotransmitters into the synaptic cleft. The fast termination of neural action requires that neurotransmitters released into the synaptic cleft are not left there to continue their action, but are removed immediately. There are two main mechanisms by which synaptic transmission is stopped as soon as the presynaptic neurones have stopped firing. First, neurotransmitter molecules are actively reabsorbed into the pre-synaptic neurone. Second, some neurotransmitter molecules are deactivated by **enzymes** in the synaptic cleft.

The first neurotransmitters to be discovered, in the 1940s, were the peripheral amines **acetylcholine** and **norepinephrine**. Acetylcholine is the transmitter between somatic nerves and muscles (which have acetylcholine receptors in their membranes), between PNS postganglionic neurones and their sites of action, and in the ganglionic synapses in both branches of the ANS. Norepinephrine is the postganglionic neurotransmitter in the SNS, acting on receptors on the target cells. In the 1950s it was established that each of these chemicals also acts as a neurotransmitter within the CNS. In the 1950s and 1960s a number of other central neurotransmitters of the amine type (e.g. **5-HT** or **serotonin**, and **dopamine**), and amino acids (like **glutamate** and **GABA**) were established. In the 1970s **peptides** such as **endorphins** were identified as central neurotransmitters. Some of these are also hormones, as we shall see later.

Why should there be so many different neurotransmitters in the central nervous system? Presumably they are there in such diversity to perform particular functions. A simple answer is that it permits synaptic transmission to be very specific. There is the possibility that transmitter molecules will 'leak' from one synapse to an adjacent one. An important characteristic of the nervous system, for functional purposes, is neural circuits; that is, how activity in one part of the brain affects activity in another. Because the brain is such a dense medium, neurones that are very close together are not necessarily functionally related to one another, so it is essential that neurotransmitters do not pass from one circuit to another, otherwise the 'wrong' circuits will be affected. This is avoided by having adjacent circuits based on different neurotransmitters. However, this is much too simple an explanation and hardly accounts for the dozens of known transmitters.

It is clear that neurotransmitters do have different effects. Some (e.g. GABA) are generally inhibitory, while others are usually excitatory. Most neurotransmitters operate by attaching to receptors in such a way as to open channels for ions to pass into and out of the neurone, thereby changing its state of polarisation. For many neurotransmitters more than one type of receptor has been identified. For example, acetylcholine has three types of receptor, two of which are excitatory and one inhibitory, norepinephrine has four types and serotonin at least six. In addition, a neurone is likely to receive inputs from many other neurones and the resulting state of polarisation of the neurone depends on the balance of excitatory and inhibitory influences. To summarise, brain function depends on the nature of the neurotransmitters involved, on the nature of the receptors, and on the location of the synapses in the brain.

The endocrine system

The hormonal, or endocrine, system generally functions as a slower-acting control system. Hormones are produced in many places in the body, including some organs called **endocrine glands,** which have as a major function the secretion of hormones. Hormones are usually (but not always) released into the blood in which they circulate to reach target cells, where they act by attaching to specific receptors (in just the same way as do neurotransmitters), producing a change in the activity of the target cells.

Hormones that interact with the nervous system are called neurohormones. These are frequently the same as substances produced by the nerves themselves, but they have a slower, longer and more widespread action. Hormones are involved in all aspects of physiology from brain development, body growth and many aspects of reproduction, through to the daily maintenance of **homeostasis** and emergency reactions. Most hormones are peptides, a few are amines and others are steroids. Because of differences in their modes of action, peptide and amine hormones produce their effects in seconds or a few minutes, while steroids do not produce effects for several minutes or hours. Conversely, the effects of peptides and amines are quickly reversed once hormone production drops, while those of steroids take a long time to diminish. Together with the fast action of the nervous system this provides enormous flexibility in control of the body.

One of the key features of the way in which the endocrine system works is that of **negative feedback**. When an endocrine gland secretes a hormone that hormone passes to target cells and produces a physiological effect. The magnitude of the effect is fed back to the endocrine gland. If the effect is too small, more hormone is produced; if it is too great, less hormone is produced. An example of this is the control of blood glucose level by **insulin**. When blood glucose is high the **pancreas** secretes insulin, which causes the removal of the glucose from the blood. The reduced level of glucose in the blood reduces the secretion of insulin. In this way the level of blood glucose is normally maintained within quite narrow limits (see Chapter 4). But one hormone does not act in isolation from the rest of the endocrine system, nor from the nervous system. Blood glucose levels, for example, are affected by other hormones, as we shall see, and by the SNS. Furthermore, in many cases, the circulating level of the hormone itself provides

TABLE 2.1 Hormones considered in this book showing their origins and effects

Gland	Hormone	Effects on
Posterior pituitary	vasopressin	water and electrolyte balance
	oxytocin	labour and lactation; male and female sexual behaviour
Anterior pituitary	luteinising hormone	ovulation; sperm and testosterone production
	follicle stimulating hormone	development of ovarian follicles; testes
	ACTH	control of adrenal cortex
	prolactin	lactation; inhibits male sexual behaviour
Adrenal medulla	epinephrine	stimulates cardiovascular function; regulates metabolism
Adrenal cortex	glucocorticoids (cortisol)	regulates metabolism in liver, muscles and adipose tissues
	mineralo-corticoids (aldosterone)	water and electrolyte balance
	androgens (testosterone)	growth and development; sex and aggression
Pancreas	insulin	energy storage; glucose uptake by cells
	glucagon	energy release
Ovaries	oestrogens (oestradiol)	female sexual differentiation
	progesterone	female sexual differentiation
Testes	androgens (testosterone)	sex differences, sex and aggression
	AMH	male sexual differentiation
Pineal	melatonin	co-ordinating body rhythms

negative feedback to control its own production, either directly, or by way of the hypothalamus and the pituitary gland.

In the remainder of this section we will look at those hormones that are important influences on the motivational states that we are concerned with in this book. These are summarised in Table 2.1.

Pituitary gland

The **pituitary gland** used to be called the master gland because it releases many hormones that act on other endocrine glands, controlling their hormone release. However, the pituitary gland is itself controlled by the hypothalamus, and this provides a clear indication of the interaction of the nervous and endocrine systems. The pituitary gland is situated immediately below the hypothalamus and has three distinct parts, which should be thought of as distinct glands. The posterior pituitary gland develops from the same tissues as the hypothalamus and can be thought of as an outgrowth of the hypothalamus. It has very rich neural connections with the **supraoptic** and **paraventricular nuclei** of the hypothalamus. Its main hormones are actually produced by neurones in the hypothalamus, and are transported along their axons to the pituitary where they are secreted into blood capillaries. These neurohormones are **vasopressin** (also called **antidiuretic hormone, ADH**), which is involved in maintaining water and **electrolyte** balance (see Chapter 3), and **oxytocin**, which is involved in lactation and in the process of labour.

The anterior pituitary gland is not neural in origin and has a circulatory rather than a neural link with the hypothalamus. This produces a variety of hormones most of which control other glands. Among these are the **gonadotropic hormones**, which cause the gonads to produce hormones (see *Ovaries* and *Testes*, pp. 31–3), **adrenocorticotropic hormone (ACTH)**, which causes the secretion of **glucocorticoids** by the **adrenal cortex** (see pp. 29–30), **prolactin**, which is involved in reproductive behaviour (see Chapter 6), and others that do not directly concern us here, including growth hormone. The secretion of each of the hormones of the anterior pituitary is under the control of releasing and inhibiting hormones produced by neurones in the hypothalamus, and transported to the pituitary in a direct blood supply that links them. The intermediate lobe of the pituitary produces one hormone, melanocyte-stimulating hormone, with which we will not be concerned.

Adrenal medulla

The adrenal glands are located immediately above the kidneys. Each adrenal gland might be considered as two more or less independent glands. The central part, the **adrenal medulla**, produces **epinephrine** (and small quantities of norepinephrine, which we saw earlier is an important SNS neurotransmitter). The adrenal medulla is sometimes viewed as a component of the SNS. Its secretory cells are analogous to the postganglionic fibres of the SNS, and are themselves innervated directly by preganglionic cells. This anatomical analogy with the SNS has a functional counterpart. Just as the SNS serves the rapid responses of the body to emergency situations, so the adrenal medulla serves longer-term emergency responses. Thus, it increases cardiac output, causes the dilatation of blood vessels in the skeletal muscles, causes the airways of the lungs to expand and increases the release of glucose and other energy-providing molecules from storage. Epinephrine and norepinephrine act through different receptor types (beta-adrenergic and alpha-adrenergic receptors respectively) so that they do not have identical physiological effects. The main control of the adrenal medulla is via the SNS, although it receives its blood supply through the adrenal cortex, and hormones released into this supply by the adrenal cortex influence epinephrine secretion in the adrenal medulla.

Adrenal cortex

Surrounding the adrenal medulla is the adrenal cortex, which produces a large number of different steroid hormones falling into three classes. Glucocorticoids, primarily **cortisol**, act primarily on glucose metabolism, but are also involved in stress reactions. Their main physiological effects support the actions of epinephrine in the release of glucose and other energy sources, and the promotion of the uptake of glucose by muscles. They also promote the breakdown of protein in muscles, which can provide a further source of energy. Finally, glucocorticoids reduce some immune system functions so they have anti-inflammatory and immunosuppressive properties. **Mineralocorticoids**, the main one of which is **aldosterone**, primarily affect electrolyte balances by actions on the kidney (see Chapter 4). **Androgens** have effects to do with sexual characteristics and behaviour after conversion to the highly active androgen **testosterone** in target organs (see Chapter 6). In men, the amount of testosterone deriving from the adrenal cortex is so small compared to that produced by the testes as to be insignificant. In women, however, most circulating androgens are secreted by the adrenal cortex and have significant effects.

The secretion of these **corticosteroids** is controlled by ACTH produced by the anterior pituitary gland. ACTH production is itself controlled by **corticotropin releasing hormone (CRH)** from the hypothalamus. In its turn, the release of CRH is affected by inputs to the hypothalamus from other brain regions. In addition, as with most hormones, the level of production of the corticosteroids is controlled by the amount of circulating corticosteroids. Thus, increased blood cortisol causes the hypothalamus and the anterior pituitary gland (both of which are outside the blood–brain barrier) to reduce production of CRH and ACTH, respectively.

Many synthetic steroids have been produced. Some of these are used therapeutically because they may have greater, more selective or longer lasting effects than naturally occurring steroids. Androgens are anabolic steroids which means that they have growth-promoting effects, including increasing muscle bulk and strength. The synthetic steroids that some athletes use (illicitly) are substances that do not occur naturally, and which are used in doses way above the concentrations at which steroids normally exist in the body. Their prolonged use can cause permanent damage to organs such as the liver and may result in premature death.

Pancreas

The pancreas has a variety of functions, all of which are related to the digestion, absorption and use of food and its products. It produces non-endocrine secretions, including enzymes that aid in the process of digestion. Its endocrine function is the secretion of four hormones, of which we will focus on two, the peptide hormones insulin and **glucagon**, which are key factors in metabolic processes controlling the storage and release of carbohydrates and fats. We will look at their functions, and the role of the pancreatic hormones in eating, in Chapter 5.

Ovaries

The ovaries, the female gonads, exert endocrine control over reproduction in females (see Chapter 6). The hormones are produced cyclically by developing follicles which also produce the ovum (see Figure 2.5). This cycle is controlled by a feedback loop involving the hypothalamus, the pituitary gland, the ovaries and the uterus. The hypothalamus produces **gonadotropin-releasing hormone (GnRH)**, which passes to the anterior pituitary, stimulating the release of **luteinising hormone (LutH)** and **follicle-stimulating hormone (FSH)**. The effects of LutH and FSH depend on the stage of the cycle. Just after menstruation, the beginning of which is conventionally Day 1 of the cycle, FSH stimulates a number of ovarian follicles to grow (the **follicular phase**). These follicles start to produce **oestrogens**, especially **oestradiol**, some of which is secreted into the blood, some being retained in the follicles. By mechanisms as yet not understood, all but one of the follicles cease to grow. The increasing oestrogen level of the blood, peaking about Day 12, stimulates LutH secretion by the pituitary, which in turn causes the follicles to reduce their oestrogen secretion and to secrete **progesterone**. It also stimulates the release by the follicle, on Day 14, of an ovum. The high level of LutH at ovulation stimulates the follicle to develop into the **corpus luteum** (the **luteal phase**). The corpus luteum secretes a large amount of progesterone and a smaller amount of oestrogen. This combination suppresses the secretion of GnRH and hence of LutH and FSH. This prevents growth of

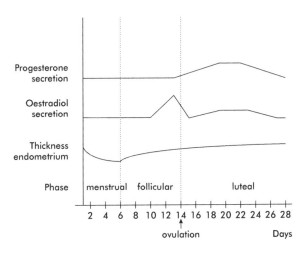

FIGURE 2.5 Hormonal and other changes during the menstrual cycle

further follicles (and is the basis of oral birth control). The corpus luteum grows for seven or eight days, then, if the ovum is not fertilised, starts to degenerate, so that after about Day 23, blood level of progesterone falls. Blood levels of LutH and FSH rise again, starting a new cycle of follicle growth.

Another of the effects of oestrogen secreted during the follicular phase is to cause the growth of the **endometrium**, the lining of the uterus. This continues during the luteal phase. If the ovum is not fertilised the drop in circulating oestrogen and progesterone causes the degeneration of the endometrium, leading to menstruation. If the ovum is fertilised it embeds itself in the endometrium and forms a placenta, which starts to secrete gonadotropic hormones. Under the influence of these, the corpus luteum does not degenerate but enlarges, continuing to secrete progesterone and oestrogen. This prevents the endometrium from degenerating and allows the foetus to develop.

Testes

The testes, the male gonads, produce primarily androgen hormones, the main one being testosterone. Testosterone is an anabolic steroid and has some effect on almost every tissue in the body. It is responsible for the embryonic differentiation of the male reproductive organs, and for the development of the secondary sexual characteristics of males at puberty. We will look in more detail at its effects in relation to sex and aggression in Chapters 6 and 7. Its secretion by the testes in the adult male is controlled by the GnRH–LutH process described above. In males, GnRH is secreted steadily rather than cyclically, as a result of a continuous negative feedback loop between the hypothalamus, the anterior pituitary gland and the testes. The testes also produce **anti-Müllerian hormone** (**AMH**), which prevents the development of female internal genitalia in male foetuses (see Chapter 6).

Pineal gland

The pineal gland, which is situated between the brain stem and the cerebral cortex, secretes **melatonin,** mainly during darkness. The effect of this hormone seems to be to match bodily rhythms with seasonal variations. In birds and some reptiles light reaches the pineal and acts directly on it. In humans the effects of light are mediated by neural connections. We shall look at the role of melatonin in Chapter 3.

Summary

The study of the psychobiology of motivation demands a general understanding of the two major control systems of the body: the nervous system and the endocrine system. This chapter presents an outline of the structure and functions of these two systems. Their particular relevance to the topics covered in the remaining chapters of this book are summarised in Figure 2.2 and Table 2.1.

Further reading

Silverthorn, D. U. (1998) *Human Physiology: An Integrated Approach,* Upper Saddle River, NJ: Prentice Hall.

Vander, A., Sherman, J. and Luciano, D. (1998) *Human Physiology: Theory, Treatment and Research*, seventh edition, Boston, MA: McGraw Hill.
There are numerous texts on human physiology, most are lavishly illustrated and all suitable for background reference for this book. The above two are good, recent examples.

Biological rhythms and sleep

L IFE IS DOMINATED BY a daily drive to fall asleep. Such rhythmicity is characteristic of animal and even plant activity. While the daily cycle of sleeping and waking is the most obvious rhythm for us, there are others, as we shall see. The importance to psychology of such rhythms is that they involve variations in motivated behaviour, emotional state and cognitive performance. For psychobiology the questions are, for example, what are the origins of these cycles? Are they driven by an internal clock? How are they influenced by external events? What are their implications for daily life? What happens if they go wrong or if we disturb them? Why do we spend about one third of our lives asleep?

Circadian rhythms

The daily sleep–waking rhythm is known as a **circadian rhythm** (meaning 'about daily'). Humans (and most other primates) are **diurnal** (meaning active in daylight), while many other animals (e.g. rodents) are **nocturnal**. The circadian rhythm is most obvious to us as a daily alternation of sleeping and waking. But it is much more than that: underlying the sleep–waking cycle are *continuous* variations in hormone secretion and metabolic activity. The latter is most clearly indicated by a daily variation in body temperature, which varies by about 1°C over the 24-hour period. This coincides with a continuous variation in cognitive capacities (e.g. ability to concentrate), which are highest when body temperature is highest. The adaptive significance of such cycles should be clear; they permit the animal to be most alert at times when it is adapted to be active. Thus, in diurnal animals, temperature and alertness are highest in the early afternoon and lowest late at night. The reverse is true of nocturnal animals.

What is the origin of these rhythms? The obvious answer, the regular alternation of day and night, is wrong. This is demonstrated by placing animals or people in isolation from the normal cues of the day–night cycle. Within one or two days of this isolation, animals and humans usually wake up and go to sleep a little later each day. This is known as a **free-running rhythm**, and in humans usually has a period of about 25 hours. This demonstrates two things: first, there is some internal (endogenous) mechanism underlying the circadian rhythm, that is some sort of biological clock with a cycle of about 25 hours; second, external events (called **Zeitgebers** from the German for time-givers) can *entrain* the circadian rhythm, normally keeping it to 24 hours. The most obvious Zeitgeber is light, and it is certainly the most important one. Other Zeitgebers have been demonstrated in hamsters, for example, social interaction, feeding and exercise. Humans use a variety of cues to help entrain the rhythm including social interaction, feeding and alarm clocks. However, light has a particular importance and I shall return to this.

Jet-lag and shift-work

In industrial societies we may engage in activities that interfere with the circadian rhythm. When we fly west, say from Manchester to New York, we move to a time zone in which sunrise occurs five hours later. Flying east from New York to Manchester, sunrise occurs five hours earlier. In each case our internal rhythm and the Zeitgebers are out of synchrony and we suffer from jet-lag, which involves sleep disturbance and diminished ability to perform activities during local waking hours. Recovery from jet-lag follows re-synchronisation of the internal rhythm and the local environment. Westward flight results in less jet-lag than eastward flight and we adjust to it more rapidly. The reasons for this are first that eastward flight results in a shorter night during the transition, and second that in order to synchronise with the new Zeitgebers, we have to try to fall asleep *later* when we have gone west but *earlier* when we have flown east. Delaying sleep onset is easier than going to sleep earlier. Adjusting fully to an eastward flight might be expected to take about one day for every hour of time shift.

The situation is similar in moving between work shifts; moving to a later shift results in less interference with performance than moving to an earlier shift. Again, the difference is that we can delay sleep onset to fit with a later activity pattern more easily than we can advance it to meet an earlier pattern. The deleterious effects of shift-work changes are best reduced by always moving to later starts. The effects of jet-lag can be minimised by preparation; in the days preceding the flight, if possible, gradually shift your waking-up time to match the time zone to which you are travelling. Alternatively (or as well), exposure to intense light early in the morning will accelerate entrainment (e.g. Boulos et al., 1995). Treatment with the hormone melatonin also promotes adjustment to such phase shifts (Deacon and Arendt, 1996).

Other biological rhythms

Circadian rhythms are not the only ones that affect us. **Ultradian** ('more than daily') **rhythms** occur more often than once per day (that is, they have a period less than 24 hours). The most important one is known as the **basic rest–activity cycle** (**BRAC**), which has a period of about 90 minutes. This rhythm was first described by Kleitman (1961) in the demand feeding schedules of newborn infants. It is seen more clearly in the cycling through different stages of sleep (see pp. 42–4). It can also be observed during waking activities as a cycle of intensity or frequency of various functions such as attention, eating, drinking and smoking; and physiological processes such as heart rate, oxygen consumption, muscle tone, gastric motility and urine production. Its effects are not obvious as it is often obscured by changes in activity and by variations in motivation (see Kleitman, 1982).

Infradian ('less than daily') **rhythms** have a period longer than 24 hours. The most obvious human example is the menstrual cycle with a period of about 28 days. Many other animals have oestrus cycles of various lengths. Another very widespread type of rhythm is **circannual rhythms**. These are clear in hibernating animals, and in the behaviour of animals and birds with an annual breeding cycle. There is now some evidence of these in humans, particularly annual cycles of depressive illness known as seasonal affective disorder (SAD).

Mechanisms of biological rhythms

We have seen that the circadian rhythm persists (at a slightly lower frequency) when people or animals are isolated from the Zeitgebers, indicating that there must be some intrinsic mechanism that provides the timing: a biological clock. Moore and Eichler (1972) and Stephan and Zucker (1972) discovered that lesions in a small area at the base of the medial hypothalamus, the **suprachiasmatic nucleus** (**SCN**), abolish rats' circadian rhythms. As the name suggests, this is immediately above the optic chiasma, which is the place in the visual pathway where the optic nerves from the two eyes come together. Although the operated rats sleep the same total amount as before the lesion, they sleep in bouts distributed throughout the day and night. The SCN lesions specifi-cally affect the *cyclicity* of sleep, not the *need* for sleep.

Other studies have shown that the SCN is the *source* of the rhythmical activity, not simply part of a pathway from elsewhere. The metabolic rate of the cells in this region is periodic (Schwartz and Gainer, 1977), and electrical recordings from isolated SCN neurones continue to show rhythmic activity that is synchronised to the light–dark cycle (Welsh *et al.*, 1995). The cellular origin of the rhythmicity is not clear, although it seems likely that it results from the synthesis of a protein that limits its own produc-tion as its concentration rises. Such a self-limiting mechanism has been shown in fruit flies, and the synthesis of one of the proteins involved is directly affected by light, permitting resetting by this Zeitgeber (e.g. Lee *et al.*, 1996). Moore (1983) discovered that the rat SCN receives information directly from the optic chiasma. Lesion studies and stimulation studies have shown that the SCN affects the entrainment of circadian rhythms. This is clearly the route through which the primary Zeitgeber, light, modulates the activity of the SCN.

Think back to the free-running experiments in which people (or animals) are isolated from all Zeitgebers. If the isolation is continued for several days, many people show an internal desynchronisation of the sleep–waking and temperature cycles. Specifically, the sleep–waking cycle tends to lengthen to around 30 hours or more, while the temperature cycle remains at about 25 hours (Aschoff, 1994). Such internal desynchronisation of sleep–waking and physiological cycles also occurs, for example, in shift workers (Motohashi, 1992). It is also known that animals presented with food at the same time each day come to anticipate it, as shown by increased activity. This effect occurs even in isolation from environmental cues and so must depend on some internal clock. This anticipation effect persists even when the SCN is destroyed. All of this suggests that there is more than one clock controlling circadian rhythms, although the other, or others, may be 'slave' clocks, normally controlled by the master clock in the SCN (see Moore-Ede, 1982).

The clock in the SCN also helps to control *infradian* rhythms. For example, many animals have an annual breeding season which commences when the day length starts to increase. Males then start to secrete more testosterone. Destruction of the SCN often abolishes this circannual cycle and animals produce constant amounts of testosterone throughout the year. However, some individual animals do not show these alterations (Zucker, Boshes and Dark, 1983). The clock in the SCN compares the relative lengths of light and dark within the 24-hour period. While the mechanisms underlying this are far from clear, the pineal gland is involved (Bartness *et al.*, 1993). Under the influence of the SCN melatonin is secreted by the pineal gland at night. Melatonin feeds back to the SCN and also affects other brain centres controlling seasonally variable processes. The greater concentration of melatonin after longer nights somehow controls these seasonal variations.

Ultradian rhythms also seem to be controlled by an endogenous clock, or clocks, although it has been suggested that they may be at least influenced by periodic variations in homeostatic behaviour such as searching for food. SCN lesions that abolish the circadian rhythms do not necessarily affect the BRAC. However, lesions in other parts of the basal hypothalamus can disrupt the BRAC, although it is not firmly established whether these are the locations of a clock or clocks, or pathways through which another mechanism affects behaviour. (Gerkema and Daan, 1985). Later, we will look at a possible midbrain location for a centre controlling the BRAC (see pp. 47–8).

The nature of sleep

Until the 1950s, sleep was viewed by many physiologists and psychologists as a state of *minimal arousal*. This fitted with the prevailing behaviourist approach in the early part of the twentieth century, according to which the main basis of motivation and emotion is general arousal. But sleep is far too complex to be described as a state of arousal. Sleep is clearly a necessity; if we are prevented from sleeping we feel tired and seek sleep. To this extent sleep may be viewed as any other motivated behaviour, with sleepiness being a subjective indication of deprivation, as are thirst and hunger. However, the nature of the deficit that sleep replaces is difficult to identify. In the following sections we will have to try to establish *why* we need to sleep, as well as *how* sleep is controlled.

Electroencephalography

The view that sleep is merely a state of low arousal changed after the discovery by Berger in 1928 that small electrical signals could be recorded from the scalp, and the demonstration that these reflected in some gross way the activity of cortical neurones. The recordings made in this way are known as **electroencephalograms**, and the machine that records them is an **electroencephalograph**. Either of these terms may be abbreviated to **EEG**. The waking EEG shows relatively fast *beta* activity (around 13–30 Hz), also called *desynchronised* EEG, when we are involved in mental activity. This is replaced by the *alpha* rhythm, or *synchronised* EEG (around 8–12 Hz), when we close our eyes and relax but are still awake. *Stage 1* sleep is characterised by slower, *theta* waves (3.5–7.5 Hz), *stage 2* by irregular, mostly slow activity, but interspersed with faster bursts (*sleep spindles*). *Stage 3* sleep shows high amplitude *delta* activity (less than 3.5 Hz), which becomes more marked in *stage 4*.

The EEG of persons falling asleep and staying asleep through the night shows a characteristic sequence (see Figure 3.1). Typically, a person cycles through this sequence throughout the night with a period of about 90 minutes, as shown in Figure 3.2. As the night progresses less time is spent in stage 4 and longer in stages 2 and 3. The initial sequence from stage 1 through to stage 4 might take only half an hour. Stages 3 and 4 together are often called *slow wave* (SW) sleep. The passage to SW sleep is accompanied by progressive slowing of the heart rate and muscular relaxation. This 90-minute cycle was the first evidence for the BRAC described on p. 38.

Rapid eye-movement sleep

After the first cycle to stage 4, occurrences of stage 1 sleep are almost always accompanied by *rapid eye movements*. This stage, called **rapid eye-movement sleep** (**REM sleep**), is associated with the deep relaxation of the muscles of the trunk found in SW sleep (although there is likely to be twitching of the muscles of the limbs and face), but with faster breathing and heart rate. Although the passage from stage 1 through to stage 4 is sometimes called 'falling more deeply asleep', the term 'deep' as applied to sleep is not very useful. REM sleep is sometimes called *paradoxical sleep* because, amongst other paradoxes, while the EEG is most similar to the waking EEG, it is always more difficult to awaken animals, and usually more difficult to awaken humans, during this stage.

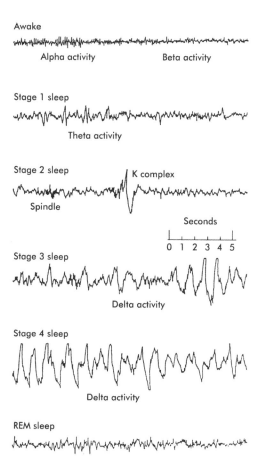

Awake

Alpha activity   Beta activity

Stage 1 sleep

Theta activity

Stage 2 sleep   K complex

Spindle

Seconds

0 1 2 3 4 5

Stage 3 sleep

Delta activity

Stage 4 sleep

Delta activity

REM sleep

FIGURE 3.1   The EEG in sleep and waking *(from Horne, 1988, by permission of Oxford University Press)*

Sleep across species

Sleep shows a clear pattern of evolution (see Kevanau, 1997). Insects, molluscs, crustaceans, amphibians and most fish, show periods of relative inactivity, but not slowing of the EEG. Most reptiles have SW sleep, but not REM sleep. Birds and mammals show both types of sleep, but different species spend different proportions of the 24 hours asleep, and different proportions of

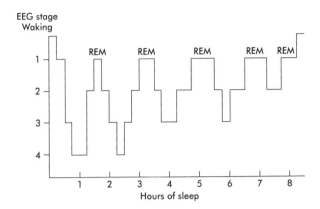

FIGURE 3.2 Typical sleep pattern through the night (after Hartmann, 1967)

that sleep time in REM sleep. Some birds and some marine mammals show SW sleep in one hemisphere, and a waking EEG in the other. There is a direct relation between body size and duration of the REM–SW sleep cycle, which is about 6 minutes in mice, 30 in cats, 90 in humans and 100 in elephants. Homeostatic control of temperature is virtually suspended during REM sleep. Since the low body weight of smaller animals means that their temperature will change more rapidly when not homeostatically controlled, they should not spend too long in REM sleep.

Development of sleep

In humans, both the total time spent sleeping and the proportion of time spent in REM sleep are greatest before birth, and decrease with age (Roffwarg, Muzio and Dement, 1966). Studies of premature infants, born between 24 and 26 weeks' gestation (14–16 weeks premature), indicate that the EEG during sleep is flat, showing only sporadic activity (e.g. Parmelee *et al.*, 1968). From then, periods of SW sleep increase, until REM and SW sleep each occupies about half of the 16 hours of sleep each day at 40 weeks (full term). From birth, the 90-minute BRAC cycle coincides with the sleep–waking cycle, and this is gradually entrained to the day–night cycle over succeeding months as the infant comes to join successive cycles together. During adulthood, the total daily length of sleep decreases, from an average of eight hours in youth down to around seven hours for humans in their fifties and sixties. The proportion of REM sleep also gradually declines, as does the amount of SW sleep, which drops from about 20 per cent at 18 years to only 2–3 per cent at 50–60 (and in some individuals may disappear altogether).

Sleep deprivation

An obvious approach to the puzzle of *why* we sleep is to deprive animals, or people, of sleep, and to observe the consequences. During total deprivation, the desire to sleep increases markedly for two or three days, so that it is difficult to keep people awake after the first 48 hours. However, sleep deprivation is accompanied by very little physiological change, and only limited cognitive changes. Performance on tasks involving reasoning, spatial relations and comprehension conducted under time constraints is usually found to be unaffected. What does deteriorate is performance of tasks involving vigilance or prolonged attention (Pilcher and Huffcutt, 1996). The effect on vigilance tasks can be partially overcome by increasing incentives. After about 60 hours of sleep deprivation hallucinations sometimes occur (e.g. Morris, Williams and Lubin, 1960). These are probably not related to psychosis because schizophrenic patients show normal sleep patterns, and their symptoms are not affected by sleep deprivation. Many of these effects might be attributable to an increasing tendency to have **microsleeps** after sleep deprivation. That is, there is an increasing tendency to have very brief periods of REM sleep whilst trying to maintain a waking state. At the end of periods of sleep deprivation, relatively little of the lost sleep is recovered; overall about 20–25 per cent is made up by longer sleep on the following two or three nights, after which the sleep period appears to return to normal. However, within this, about 70 per cent of SW and 50 per cent of REM sleep is recovered.

When sleep deprivation was extended beyond what has been possible voluntarily in humans, experimental rats died after about 4 weeks (Rechtschaffen *et al.*, 1983). The sleep-deprived animals did not show any specific pathological changes, but rather showed the general changes, at least partly attributable to deficits in immune system function, that are found following exposure to any prolonged stressor, including enlarged adrenal glands, stomach ulcers and internal haemorrhages. While voluntary sleep deprivation never has these effects in humans, there is a rare pathological condition, *fatal familial insomnia*, which causes sufferers suddenly to stop sleeping in middle age. These people die and show general physical effects similar to those of the sleep-deprived rats, together with degeneration in the thalamus which may be the cause of the sleep loss (Sforza *et al.*, 1995).

The effects on humans of *selective deprivation of REM sleep* have also been studied. If people are awoken as soon as their EEG shows that they are entering REM sleep, the effect on the sleep pattern is immediate. From the first night subjects enter REM sleep with increasing frequency, and this might increase to as many as 50 times in one night (Dement, 1960). Thus, there seems to be a real drive to enter REM sleep. When, at the end of the deprivation period, subjects are allowed to sleep uninterrupted, they spend as much as twice the usual amount of time in REM sleep, even though the overall length of sleep is hardly increased. There appear to be no persistent psychological effects of REM-sleep deprivation that are different from those of general loss of sleep (Greenberg, Pillard and Pearlman, 1972).

Dreaming

Kleitman (1961) discovered that people woken during REM periods almost always report vivid dreams. Waking in non-REM periods results either in no dream reports or in vague, easily lost reports. Dreams run in real-time: REM periods last up to 40 minutes, and people awoken at different points will give approximately accurate reports of the duration of the dream they have been awoken from. People who claim that they never dream have just as many REM-sleep periods as others, and they are nearly as likely to report dreams when awoken during these periods. Long-term memory traces of the dreams are apparently not formed during sleep, so they are mostly not recalled on waking. Those that are recalled are those we awaken during, or shortly after. External stimuli can become incorporated into the dream. For example, the alarm clock becomes a bell in the dream.

Many have argued that dreaming serves important psychological functions and that we sleep in order to dream. We will look at this in the final section of this chapter.

Mechanisms of sleep

Brémer argued in 1936 that consciousness is maintained by diffuse sensory input to the cortex, and that sleep results from *reduced sensory input*. Transection of the brain stem above the pons in cats resulted in a continuous sleeping EEG. Transection below the brain stem did not disrupt the normal sleep–waking cycle. Brémer argued that the difference was that the higher lesion cut sensory input to the cortex. Moruzzi and Magoun (1949) demonstrated that stimulation of the brain stem reticular formation results in EEG arousal and behavioural excitation, while lesions there cause prolonged sleep. This ascending **reticular activating system (RAS)** is now known to activate cells in the thalamus that project generally to the cortex, producing the alert EEG. In turn, the cortex sends information back to these portions of the thalamus forming the *thalamocortical loop*. This positive feedback system is controlled by various inhibitory connections from, for example, the **raphé nuclei** in the brain stem. At sleep onset, the activity of the RAS decreases, eventually to a point where it generates insufficient inhibition to damp the feedback circuits, so that large-amplitude, slow, co-ordinated activity results which prevents stimulus processing and results in sleep. Precisely why and how this process starts is not known, although the **preoptic area** of the basal forebrain is involved. Lesions here cause cats to stop sleeping (e.g. Szymusiak and McGinty, 1989), and stimulation induces SW sleep in cats (Sterman and Clemente, 1962). Since the preoptic area is adjacent to the SCN which, as we have seen, is the location of the master circadian clock, it is likely that fibres from the SCN pass to the pre-optic area to entrain sleeping and waking to a circadian cycle.

After about an hour of sleep the RAS becomes active again, returning us to faster EEG activity accompanied by REM. Neurones in an area of the pons, the **peribrachial area**, become increasingly active before the onset of REM sleep, and show a high rate of firing throughout REM periods (El Mansari, Sakai and Jouvet, 1989). Destruction of the cell bodies of these neurones almost eliminates REM sleep, showing that they have a controlling function (Webster and Jones, 1988). The axons of these neurones pass to various centres, controlling the different aspects of the REM state. Those passing to the pontine reticular formation, the preoptic area and the thalamus are responsible for the alert cortical EEG (Siegel, 1989). Rapid eye-movements are produced by centres in the tectum of the midbrain, which also receive axons from the peribrachial area (Webster and Jones, 1988). Axons passing to the lateral geniculate nucleus in the thalamus control the appearance of **PGO waves** (from Pons, Geniculate and Occiput whence they may be recorded), which seem to act as powerful internal stimuli, producing bursts of activity in sensory areas of the cortex (Sakai and Jouvet, 1980). Those passing to the subcoerulear nucleus in the pons produce muscular relaxation by stimulating cells in the medulla that in turn inhibit motor neurones in the spinal cord (Shouse and Siegel, 1992).

There have been *chemical theories* about the control of sleep. A number of experiments early in this century demonstrated that the injection of fluids either from sleeping or sleep-deprived animals can lead to sleep in non-deprived animals. This led to the supposition that sleep results from a build-up of some chemical substance in the body. A number of possible sleep-promoting sub-stances have been identified over the years, including melatonin. As we have seen, melatonin levels rise during darkness. It affects circadian rhythms, and in other species appears to act as a factor promoting the entrainment of rhythmic activities, especially the secretion of sex hormones, to light–dark cycles. It does not act as a sleep-promoting substance, except in very high doses (Mishima *et al.*, 1997), but it has been used to treat sleep disturbances, which it seems to do by helping the entrainment of sleep to the daily light–dark cycle (de Vries and Peeters, 1997). One good reason for believing that circulating substances do *not* control sleep in humans comes from a study by Webb (1978) of conjoined ('Siamese') twins who shared a circulatory system. Their sleeping and waking periods were found not to be co-ordinated.

Functions of sleep

Many theories have been proposed to explain the function or functions of sleep. The main types of theory can be described as either *recuperative* or *circadian*. Recuperative views either regard sleep as a period during which repair processes take place, or during which processes related to learning occur. Circadian approaches suggest that sleep evolved as a way of fitting organisms to the light–dark cycle, conserving energy for those times of the day when they need to be active to seek food, mates and so on. One problem with such a general approach is that REM sleep is maladaptive in the homeostatic sense, since, as I have pointed out, temperature control ceases.

It is difficult to find in any of the preceding information any convincing function for non-REM sleep, apart from a general restorative function. Some studies have indicated that vigorous exercise selectively increases SW sleep (see Horne, 1981), but others have shown no such effect (Horne, 1981). Horne and Harley (1989) have argued that the inconsistencies may be explained by the effects of the exercise on the body. Specifically, exercise that raises the temperature of the brain increases SW sleep. They demonstrated this by showing that local heating of the head without exercise increased subsequent SW sleep. It is interesting to note that the basal forebrain areas that control sleep are also involved in temperature regulation. Further, other situations that raise body temperature, such as fever and hot weather, induce sleepiness.

As far as REM sleep is concerned, *developmental theories* emphasise the predominance of REM sleep early in development, and suggest, for example, that it plays a key role in brain development; perhaps by promoting synaptic connections (e.g. Roffwarg, Muzio and Dement, 1966). *Learning theories* propose that REM sleep permits or at least promotes the formation of long-term memories (Greenberg and Pearlman, 1974). Early in this century claims were made that a period of sleep following learning improves memory. However, such claims are now treated with caution. First, the apparent enhancement of memory by sleep might be a *passive* outcome owing to reduced retroactive interference from later stimulation rather than an *active* process of memory formation or consolidation. Second, the effect, when it is shown at all, is small (see Smith, 1985). However, in a more recent review of work on rats and humans, Smith (1995) concluded that deprivation of REM sleep is detrimental to memory of responses in rats as long as it takes place in a narrow 'window' shortly after the acquisition of the response. In humans REM-sleep deprivation has no effect on explicit learning (consciously learned facts, events or stimuli), but does impair *implicit learning* (formation of memories of which we are not necessarily aware without effort; for example, a stimulus seen once will influence later recognition tasks).

A view of the origin of sleep that is receiving much attention now is that it serves to maintain and enhance *synaptic efficiency*. Roffwarg, Muzio and Dement (1966) argued that the SW–REM sleep cycle evolved to allow the repetitive activation of neural circuits: dynamic stabilisation. This activation essentially allows the circuits to develop and keeps them ready for use. Kevanau (1997) has recently described the elaboration of this theory and has reviewed the evidence for it. Primitive animals merely need periods of rest, including decreased muscle tone, to effect dynamic stabilisation. As evolution produced greater brain complexity, so the need for dynamic stabilisation became greater and necessitated primitive (SW) sleep to isolate the brain from sensory processing. The later evolution of **endothermy** (the ability to maintain body temperature) meant that SW sleep was not sufficient to prevent more vigorous muscle contractions that might result from dynamic stabilisation from interfering with the process. For this reason REM sleep evolved, actively inhibiting sensory and motor connections of the brain, as we have seen. The different EEG rhythms of the sleep stages represent stimulation of neural circuits in different brain structures. Thus, for example, the theta rhythms of REM sleep act on primitive mechanisms in the hippocampus. The reason REM sleep is so prominent in the foetus is because that is when most of these circuits are being formed. The high amplitude, slower EEG of SW sleep reflects the same process in cortical association areas.

None of these theories pays much attention to dreaming. Dreams might simply be meaningless by-products of the sensory activation described above, or of memory consolidation processes. Others have viewed dreams as the important component of sleep. Freud (1915) and his followers, of course, viewed dreams as a 'safe' way in which the individual could express (in a disguised manner) repressed drives. Sleep could be viewed as existing largely to serve this function. A version of this sort of view has modern adherents. Cartwright (1989), for example, regards sleep as existing for the purpose of allowing us to resolve emotional problems during dreams. Since it is impossible to deprive somebody of dreams without also depriving them of REM sleep, and *vice versa*, it is impossible to decide whether dreams are the key component of sleep, or merely a by-product.

Summary

Like that of other animals human behaviour is rhythmical. Daily (circadian) rhythms fit the organism to the light–dark cycle, and involve cycles of metabolic and endocrine activity, as well as motivated behaviour and cognitive function. Circadian rhythms are generated by an internal (biological) clock in the suprachiasmatic nucleus of the hypothalamus, which free-running studies show has a period of about 25 hours. This is entrained to the light–dark cycle by way of direct pathways from the retina to the hypothalamus.

We are also subject to ultradian rhythms (such as the basic rest–activity cycle, of about 90 minutes) and infradian rhythms (such as the menstrual cycle, of about 28 days). These other rhythms are, at least *partially*, independent of the clock in the suprachiasmatic nucleus. Sleep demonstrates cycles of slow and fast EEG activity, with a period of about 90 minutes. Fast EEG periods are associated with rapid eye movements, and are the time when clear dreams occur. Only endothermic animals seem to show this cyclical type of sleep. In human infants, REM sleep occupies about half of the 24-hour cycle before birth, and the proportion drops markedly throughout post-natal life. Sleep deprivation has little effect on cognitive tasks except those involving vigilance. Sleep results from a decrease in activity in the ascending reticular activating system, which permits the thalamocortical loop to produce large, slow waves of activity. During sleep there is active inhibition of sensory and motor connections to the brain. The function of sleep is still unclear. One current theory is that it takes the brain 'off-line' in order that dynamic stabilisation (consolidation) of neural networks can take place. Others view sleep as permitting dreams to resolve emotional problems.

Further reading

Hobson, J. A. (1989) *Sleep*, New York: Scientific American Library. This book provides a fairly concise general overview of sleep research.

Kevanau, J. L. (1997) 'Origin and evolution of sleep: roles of vision and endothermy', *Brain Research Bulletin*, 42: 245–64. This paper gives an authoritative and readable account of a major current theory of sleep. In the process of doing so, it includes a lot of information about the evolutionary and human development of sleep.

Kryger, M. H., Roth, T. and Dement, W. C. (eds) (1989) *Principles and Practice of Sleep Medicine*, Philadelphia, PA: W. B. Saunders. Despite its title, almost half of this book is concerned with providing a comprehensive account of the nature, origins and mechanisms of normal sleep and dreaming, as well as chapters on circadian rhythms. The second half of the book covers abnormalities of sleep, including jet-lag and shift-work.

Chapter 4

Homeostasis and drinking

Homeostasis

Animal cells and organs will only work optimally when their operating environment is maintained within a very narrow range of conditions. We have physiological mechanisms for controlling many aspects of the internal environment to provide optimal conditions for temperature, electrolyte concentrations, pH (acidity) of body fluids, oxygen level, carbohydrate concentrations of tissues and so on. The physiological process that produces this stability in the face of fluctuations in the demands that the environment makes on the body is known as homeostasis, a term introduced by Walter Cannon in 1929.

Homeostasis operates through negative feedback. The operation of such a system is often likened to the operation of thermostatically controlled heating systems. As we shall see the analogy is a poor one, although it does serve to illustrate the basic principles of negative feedback control.

Negative feedback systems

The essential features of such a control system are as shown in Figure 4.1. First, there is a *system variable*, which is the property that is to be controlled. In the case of a thermostat this is room temperature. Second, there is a **set point,** which is the target value of the property, in this case a temperature which the system tries to maintain. Third, the system needs a *sensor*, in this example, this would be some form of thermometer, to detect and report the current state of the system to, fourth, a *comparator*, which tests if the system variable is different from the set point. Fifth, the system needs a *control*, a mechanism to start and stop the sixth feature, which is a *correctional process*. In a thermostatic system, these are respectively a switch and a heater. Frequently,

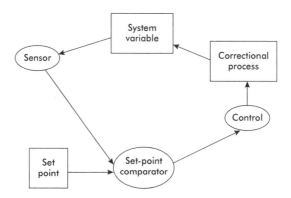

FIGURE 4.1   A simple negative feedback control system

the sensor, set-point comparator and the control will be combined. For example, in a room thermostat, the sensor might be a bi-metallic strip which bends when the temperature rises and falls, switching a heater on and off. Such a control system is described as a negative feedback system because increases in the system variable feed back to the control to switch off the correctional process. In the case of a room heater, when the sensor detects that the temperature has fallen below the set point, it causes a switch to start a heater, which causes the temperature to rise. When the thermometer detects that the temperature has risen above the set point, it causes the switch to stop the heater.

Now, a simple system like a room thermostat has a number of disadvantages which might be merely inconvenient in controlling room temperature, but which could be fatal in a homeostatic mechanism. First, the physical nature of thermostats determines that they cannot maintain an exact temperature. Instead, the temperature at which they switch the heater on is always lower than the temperature at which they switch it off. Usually, this difference is quite large, as you can tell for yourself by turning the control on a room thermostat up and then down. You will hear the click of the switch turning on and off at different positions on the thermostat. In a physiological system this could lead to an unacceptably wide variation in metabolic efficiency. It is possible to improve on this by having a heater that is capable of a continuously variable output, which is controlled by detected variations in temperature. Such a system is a *servo* system, but it retains the essential characteristic of working on the basis of negative feedback. Physiological control systems are more like servos.

A second limitation of a simple thermostatically controlled heating system is that it permits correction only in one direction. That is, if the temperature rises above the set point, there is no way to lower it. This can be overcome by adding another correctional process that would cool the room if it gets too hot, and we can do this with air conditioning, which again would operate as a negative feedback system. This, too, is a feature of physiological control. A third difficulty with the room heater analogy is that it is vulnerable to failure of components or of the connections between them. If any one of these fails, the whole system fails. The solution to this is to build redundancy into the control system, by having more than one of each component, preferably with more than one connection between components. It would also be an advantage if the correctional processes were of different types, which would permit the system to cope if, for example, one source of energy failed. For similar reasons we might expect to find that there are *satiety mechanisms*, separate from the mechanism that starts the correction, to stop the correctional process. Both of these are characteristic of homeostatic systems.

Homeostatic behaviour

Mammals and other endotherms, mostly birds, are able to maintain temperature within a very narrow range that is optimal for biochemical activity, and hence physiological processes. Other groups of animals, **ectotherms**, such as reptiles and amphibians, cannot control their own body temperature by internal mechanisms. The metabolism of ectotherms slows down when the environment gets colder, and speeds up when it gets warmer. The only ways that they have of controlling temperature are behavioural. To increase their body temperature they will seek sunlight and orient their bodies to maximise their absorption of heat. To cool themselves they will seek shade. Mammals also engage in such behaviour (for example, usually preferring to rest in warmer parts of the environment). In general, we shall refer to behaviours that promote homeostasis as **homeostatic behaviour.** We will see that, as in the case of temperature control, the control of other physiological states is accomplished by a combination of physiological homeostatic mechanisms and homeostatic behaviour.

Fluid regulation

Just as body temperature needs to be maintained within narrow limits, so we need to control the amount of water contained in our bodies. First, the total *volume* of water in the body needs to be controlled because some physical processes, in particular the circulation of the blood, require the maintenance of volume and pressure within a narrow range. Second, the biochemical reactions that are the basis of life depend on the reacting substances being within a particular range of concentrations, just as they depend on body temperature being maintained within a narrow range. Certain bodily processes, including some involved in temperature regulation, sweating and breathing, as well as others such as the excretion of urine, involve a net loss of water from the body. Some of these processes lose only water (e.g. breathing), while others involve the loss of electrolytes, particularly sodium and chloride ions, as well as water (e.g. sweating, bleeding, urination).

The biochemical processes mentioned above take place within cells, and it is the electrolytes in the **intracellular fluid** within these cells that have to be maintained at a constant concentration. The intracellular fluid is separated from the **interstitial fluid** (the fluid immediately surrounding all cells) by complex membranes. As we saw in Chapter 2, these membranes contain receptors for various chemical substances, but they also have a property described as **semipermeable.** Cell membranes strongly resist the passage of certain inorganic **ions,** such as sodium, while freely permitting the passage of water molecules and waste products of cellular metabolism. Normally the intracellular and extracellular fluids are isotonic. That is, the various fluids maintain a balance of concentration of dissolved substances (solutes) inside and outside the cells. If the concentration of a solute inside a cell rises it becomes hypertonic, and water will pass into the cell to re-establish the equilibrium. Similarly, if the concentration within the cell falls and it becomes hypotonic, water will pass out of the cell until the intracellular and extracellular fluids are again isotonic. This process is called osmosis.

In addition to permitting the passage of food, waste and other substances such as some hormones into and out of cells, the interstitial fluid may be described as acting as a buffer. It permits the immediate correction of the electrolyte concentration of the cells, so that the essential biochemical processes may continue. In turn, the interstitial fluid is in contact, through semipermeable membranes, with the blood plasma in the capillaries. Therefore, in order for ingested water to influence the intracellular fluid, it has to be absorbed from the gastrointestinal tract into the blood stream, and from there into the interstitial fluid.

It should be clear that the control of water in the body must be closely connected with the control of electrolytes, and particularly of sodium. Normally we ingest far more water and far more sodium ions (mostly from common salt) than we need. As mentioned previously, some of the ways in which we lose water from the body also involve the loss of electrolytes, while others do not. The way in which we normally lose most water, and most excess sodium, is by urination. We also lose significant amounts of water and sodium through sweating, and through haemorrhage, both following trauma and through menstruation. The amount lost through sweating rises enormously during exercise and also when the temperature, either environmental or body, rises.

The major route of water loss that does not also lose electrolytes is evaporation, mainly through breathing but also through the skin. Water is also lost through defecation. None of the processes that lose water can be completely switched off (for example, we have to produce urine to get rid of waste products), which means that water needs to be replaced to maintain blood volume and pressure, and to maintain cellular electrolyte concentrations. The question we must consider now is: what are the mechanisms that control this replacement of water? In the following sections we will explore the physiological mechanisms that appear to provide negative feedback control of water and electrolyte balance, trying as we do so to identify the components of such homeostatic systems outlined earlier. We will then examine the extent to which drinking in humans is explained by these mechanisms.

Thirst and drinking

Thirst, the conscious sensation of needing to drink water, only occurs if the body reaches a state of deficit. We normally drink as a matter of habit, for example with meals, or we anticipate exceptional water requirements and drink more, for example before playing sports on a hot day. Furthermore, homeostatic processes normally keep the fluid and electrolyte balances of the body very closely controlled. Thirst is usually experienced after such events as exercise, after ingesting common salt or diuretic substances such as alcohol, or after sudden blood loss. Even in the last case the blood loss needs to be severe, since blood donors, who lose about 10 per cent of their blood volume, do not usually report thirst.

Earlier, I mentioned two physiological reasons for replacing lost water. The first is the biophysical need to maintain blood volume and pressure. Second, there is the biochemical need to maintain cellular electrolyte concentrations. These two distinct needs to replace water suggest that there might be two mechanisms acting to replace water lost in two different ways: through loss of water only (mainly through evaporation); and through loss of isotonic fluids (urination, sweating, vomiting and bleeding). This, in turn, gives us clues to the two sensory mechanisms involved. The first is based on loss of water volume and would most likely be stimulated by loss of blood.

Hypovolaemic thirst

The mechanism proposed to result from volume loss is called *hypovolaemic* (or sometimes *volumetric)* thirst. The existence of this as a separate system is demonstrated by withdrawing blood or by the injection into the abdominal cavity of substances (colloids) that draw plasma from the blood, both of which cause a rapid decrease in the volume of the extracellular fluid. Neither of these changes the electrolyte balance of the body, yet each results in increased drinking (Fitzsimons, 1961). The immediate consequences of loss of blood volume are lowered blood pressure and reduced blood flow through the body. The body possesses specialised receptors for each of these changes, each of which plays a role in hypovolaemic thirst, as well as in immediate neural correction of the lowered blood pressure. *Blood-flow receptors* in the kidneys detect a decrease in blood flow and secrete **renin** into the blood. Renin initiates a sequence of biochemical changes which result in the circulation of a hormone, **angiotensin**. This has a number of physiological effects: it causes peripheral **vaso-constriction** (producing an immediate increase in blood pressure), it causes the adrenal cortex to secrete the hormone aldosterone (which produces salt retention by the kidneys), and it stimulates the posterior pituitary gland to secrete vasopressin (ADH), which causes water retention by the kidneys.

The second type of specialised receptors for lowered blood volume are **baroreceptors** located in the walls of the atria of the heart. These are stretch receptors that detect how much blood is returning to the heart; the lower the volume of returning blood, the less the receptors are stretched. Physiologists have long believed that these baroreceptors function, in combination with similar receptors in the main arteries leaving the heart, to control blood pressure. In more recent years research by Fitzsimons and colleagues (e.g. Fitzsimons and Moore-Gillon, 1980) has shown that reducing the amount of blood reaching the heart (by partially inflating a balloon in the vena cava, the vein that returns blood to the right atrium) results in drinking. Conversely, stimulating the baroreceptors by stretching them directly with an inflated balloon results in reduced drinking. Chemical blocking of angiotensin receptors does not affect these results, indicating that the effect is independent of renin production by the kidneys.

The second physiological mechanism for the control of fluid balance is based on *cellular dehydration*. As water is lost from the body the interstitial fluid is no longer able to replace water in the cells. This leads to *osmotic* (or *osmometric*) *thirst* and increased drinking. A simple way to demonstrate this is to ingest salt (for example, in the form of salted peanuts such as those given away in bars). The result is a higher concentration in the interstitial fluid producing diffusion of water out of cells. This results in increased drinking (and in increased turnover for the bar).

The process described happens to all cells, but it is now known that there are cells in several parts of the brain that respond specifically to hypertonicity by passing signals to other areas, and we will look at this in a moment. Earlier research suggested that these **osmoreceptors** are located in the *anterior lateral hypothalamus* (Andersson, 1953) and the *lateral preoptic area* (Peck and Blass, 1975). However, more recent studies have cast doubt on this (e.g. Andrews *et al.*, 1992), and others have shown that the osmoreceptors are situated in and around the **organum vasculosum of the lamina terminalis** (**OVLT**), a nearby area in the circumventricular organs (adjacent to the third ventricle) which is outside the blood–brain barrier (Buggy *et al.*, 1979). There are also osmoreceptors in the throat, the stomach and the liver which do not result in immediate drinking. Rather, they operate through a different feedback loop that releases vasopressin, which, as we have already noted, causes water retention in the kidneys.

We have autonomic, hormonal and behavioural means of controlling electrolyte and water balance. The neural mechanisms for the control of drinking are complex and not fully understood. A simplified description of the main centres and pathways is shown in Figure 4.2. Lesions in the **subfornical organ** (**SFO**), one of the circumventricular organs, stop the normal drinking response to

61

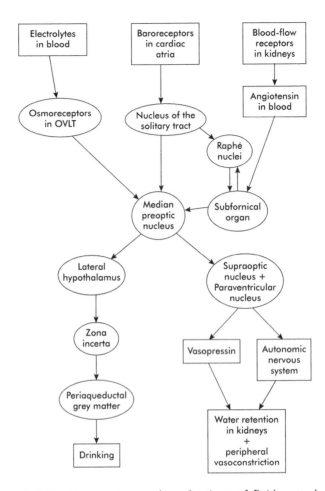

FIGURE 4.2 Main centres and mechanisms of fluid control

weak hypertonic solutions (Simpson, Epstein and Camardo, 1978). As we have seen the OVLT contains osmoreceptors. These circumventricular organs are richly supplied by blood vessels and are effectively outside the blood–brain barrier. They seem to be adapted to respond to hormones in, and hypertonicity of, the blood. Angiotensin produced after stimulation of blood-flow receptors in the kidneys attaches to receptors in the SFO. These areas communicate through connections with other parts of the brain, including the posterior pituitary gland, promoting the secretion of vasopressin (with effects already noted), and to areas of the hypothalamus which control the autonomic nervous system. The behavioural effects seem to involve a mechanism in which axons from the SFO and the OVLT terminate in the **median preoptic nucleus (MPN)** (Lind and Johnson, 1982). The MPN also receives direct sensory inputs from the baroreceptors in the atria of the heart. Thus, the same control and effector mechanisms apply to volumetric thirst and osmotic thirst.

The lateral hypothalamus and the lateral preoptic area seem not to be themselves osmoreceptive, but pass information to the **zona incerta,** in the midbrain reticular formation. The zona incerta is connected with a number of brain structures concerned with the control of motivated behaviours, including the **periaqueductal grey matter.** In some, as yet unknown, way this results in drinking.

Tanaka *et al.* (1998) have argued that a key role in fluid control is played by neural networks between the *raphé nuclei,* which we saw in Chapter 3 are also involved in the maintenance of arousal, and the SFO. Loss of blood volume stimulates the **parabrachial nucleus (PBN)** and the **nucleus of the solitary tract (NST),** both of which are sites for the reception in the CNS of autonomic afferent information. These pass information to the raphé nuclei, which have serotonergic connections with the SFO. In turn, the SFO monitors angiotensin in the blood, and communicates with the dorsal raphé nuclei, with angiotensinergic neurones.

It may be seen from this brief account that the mechanisms that control drinking are intimately related to the autonomic control of fluid homeostasis. Furthermore, the mechanisms involve activity in numerous neural structures and many different neurotransmitters. Research continues to provide further detail about these mechanisms.

Satiety mechanisms

The one step missing from these descriptions of the mechanisms that control drinking is satiety mechanisms. The systems we have looked at would have a considerable lag before they can change the system sufficiently to stop ingestion. For example, drinking stops several minutes before the ingested water passes from the gastrointestinal tract to re-hydrate the extracellular fluid (Ramsay, Rolls and Wood, 1977). Despite this humans and animals drink just about the right amount of water to correct any deficit. The obvious nature and location of such a satiety mechanism would be osmoreceptors in the mouth. In the same way that we locate our sensation of thirst primarily in the mouth, so wetting of the mouth should indicate to us that we can stop drinking. Indeed, wetting the mouth does quench our thirst temporarily. If rats are given surgically a fistula to carry water out of the oesophagus before it reaches the stomach, and are then made thirsty and allowed to drink, they cease drinking immediately they wet their mouths but then quickly resume and drink enormous amounts of water. This brief cessation of drinking does not occur if the same quantity of water is introduced through a tube directly into the stomach. This suggests that there are two satiety mechanisms. One is a short-term mechanism which is strongest in the mouth and weakest further down the gastrointestinal tract. The other is a long-term mechanism based on the osmoreceptors in the throat, in later parts of the gastrointestinal tract and in the liver. These, as we have seen, inhibit vasopressin secretion when stimulated by water. Passing water into different levels of the gastrointestinal tract in animals has shown that the long-term inhibitory effect on drinking increases the further down the tract the water is introduced. (See Verbalis, 1991, for a review of the processes of satiation.)

Non-deficit drinking in humans

As I stated earlier, these homeostatic mechanisms normally prevent us reaching a state of water deficit sufficient to produce thirst. Most of the preceding discussion has been about such deficit-induced drinking, and does not necessarily tell us how we, as human beings, normally behave to avoid getting into extreme deficits. The main danger of the drug ecstasy seems to be that its behavioural effects lead to loss of both water and electrolytes (through sweating), which the users may not anticipate or notice (Squier *et al.*, 1995). These effects may be avoided by the same strategy used by athletes, namely drinking isotonic drinks. The fact is that we normally do not wait until we are deprived before drinking. Phillips *et al.* (1984) showed that humans given free access to water throughout a normal working day reported variations in thirst, perceived dryness of the mouth and pleasantness of the taste of water which were not associated with any change in any relevant physiological variables.

Booth (1991) has summarised the factors that influence human drinking. Drinking has **positive incentive properties**. That is, it is nice to do and that is why we do it. Often we drink because the liquid we are drinking is used to carry other substances into the body, active agents such as alcohol or caffeine, or simply because the drink tastes nice (see also Gilbert, 1991). With increasing deprivation, and hence thirst, we prefer drinks with less flavour and with lower concentrations of sugars, salts and so on. Conversely, studies with human beings under conditions leading to dehydration have shown that if the water available is made unpalatable, people will not drink enough to re-hydrate their tissues fully (Engell and Hirsch, 1991). Consumption is influenced by the temperature of the drink so that any particular drink will have a particular temperature range that provides maximal motivation to drink it. This optimal temperature will depend on a variety of sensory factors (so that, for example, many white wines are preferred at low temperatures and red wines at higher temperature) as well as cultural ones (Booth suggests that the optimal temperature for beer is higher in the UK than in the USA.) Finally, drinking is affected by social factors so that individual desire to drink is higher when more people are drinking. What is more, when drinking socially, we frequently choose drinks containing alcohol. Since alcohol is itself a diuretic (that is, it causes increased urination), this stimulates further drinking to replace the additional lost water.

Summary

The internal environment is maintained close to optimal conditions by the physiological process of homeostasis assisted by homeostatic behaviour. Homeostasis operates through negative feedback and explanations of the control of fluid balance, as other physiologically based motivations, have been based on the same principles. Drinking results from a reduction in blood volume or from changes in electrolyte balance. The mechanisms that control these have both peripheral and central components, and are based on numerous neurotransmitters. The mechanisms are highly redundant and work in concert with autonomic and endocrine systems maintaining fluid and electrolyte homeostasis. Drinking is also stimulated by eating and, as in other circumstances, is subject to learning, so that drinking does not always, or even usually, result from actual tissue deficits. Water has positive incentive properties and drinking is affected by a variety of sensory, social and cultural factors.

Further reading

Ramsay, D. J. and Booth, D. A. (eds) (1991) *Thirst: Physiological and Psychological Aspects*, London: Springer-Verlag. The 31 chapters in this book cover all of the main approaches to the study of drinking in animals and humans from psychophysics to neuro-chemistry.

Valle, F. P. (1995) 'A reexamination of the role of associative factors in the control of "normal drinking" in the rat', in R. Wong (ed.) *Biological Perspectives on Motivated Activities*, Norwood, NJ: Ablex Publishing Co., pp. 289–335. Concentrates on the non-physiological factors, both learned and sensory, that are important in the control of drinking, even in rats.

Chapter 5

Hunger and eating

Food

Food serves a number of requirements of the body. Each of the three main food groups (**macronutrients**), carbohydrates, proteins and fats, provides energy. In addition, food provides the body with a variety of other nutrients. Proteins provide the key building blocks of tissues, **amino acids,** some of which cannot be synthesised by the body. Fats (in general, **lipids**) are also important in numerous physiological processes and some fats, the *essential fatty acids*, cannot be synthesised in the body. Most vitamins, and all of the minerals that are essential for the proper functioning of the body, must be ingested in the diet. By the process of digestion food is broken down mechanically and chemically into simpler substances that are absorbed from the small intestines and used by the cells of the body.

Energy use and storage

The tissues of the body obtain most of their energy from the metabolism of *glucose* or of *free fatty acids*. Energy requirements are continuous, but food intake is occasional, so most of the energy in ingested food is stored. Immediately before eating, during digestion (in response to the secretion by the stomach and intestines of gastrointestinal hormones) and during absorption (following stimulation of **glucoreceptors** in the liver by increased blood glucose), insulin is released from the pancreas. Amongst its metabolic effects, insulin causes glucose to be stored in the liver in the form of a more complex molecule, **glycogen**. As circulating glucose is used by the tissues another pancreatic hormone, glucagon, causes the reconversion of glycogen to glucose and its release into the bloodstream. Blood glucose levels are maintained within quite narrow limits by the dynamic negative feedback loops provided by these hormones.

Only a small proportion (about 800 Calories) of ingested energy is stored in this immediately available way, mostly in the muscles, but some in the liver. Most glucose is converted into fatty acids and hence into fats in the liver and in **adipose tissues**. Most of this fat is kept as a longer term store in the adipose tissues, and in an average-weight person may amount to some 140,000 Calories. All of these storage processes are promoted by insulin. When glycogen levels in the liver fall, this stored fat begins to be mobilised, again under the influence of glucagon, by conversion into fatty acids and glucose.

Control systems

Most studies of the control of eating have concerned the control of energy supply. When we need to eat we feel hungry. Just as thirst indicates a deficit of water, so hunger indicates a deficit of food. We will start our search for the mechanisms involved in the control of eating by examining first what might seem to be an obvious place.

Gastric contractions

The first theory of hunger was proposed in 1929 by Cannon and Washburn. After conducting experiments recording the movements of the stomach, they concluded that eating follows hunger signalled by gastric contractions which result from the stomach being empty, and ceases when food reaches the stomach, stopping these hunger contractions. However, this is not a sufficient explanation. First, surgical removal of the stomach in humans does not prevent feelings of hunger, and patients maintain normal body weight by eating more, smaller meals. Second, cutting the nerves between the stomach and the central nervous system does not affect food intake nor reports of hunger in humans.

Dual-centre set-point theory

Mayer (1953) proposed a *glucostatic theory*, stating that the signal for eating to start is a drop of the blood glucose level below a set point. Eating ceases when the level rises to reach that point again. In each case the sensors for blood glucose levels were proposed to be glucoreceptors in the brain. Destruction of such glucoreceptors in rats by the injection of *gold thioglucose*, which binds to them and then, being neurotoxic, kills them, resulted in **hyperphagia** (overeating); the rats ate until they became extremely obese. Subsequent histology of the rats' brains revealed that the destroyed cells were in the ventromedial nucleus of the hypothalamus (the **ventromedial hypothalamus, VMH**). Mayer labelled this area a **satiety centre** for eating. The identification of a satiety centre in the VMH is supported by clinical studies of persons with tumours in this region, who may develop hyperphagia.

So, if there is a satiety centre in the brain, is there also a centre to control the *start* of feeding? Anand and Brobeck (1951) showed that bilateral lesions in the *lateral hypothalamus* (LH) produced **aphagia** (failure to eat), and they concluded that this was a feeding centre that controls the commencement of eating. Subsequent studies showed that electrical stimulation of the LH can produce eating. Following this, in the 1950s and 1960s, the predominant view of the control of eating was the *dual-centre set-point model*, suggesting, in short, that eating commences with the stimulation of the LH feeding centre by a fall in blood glucose level below a set point, and ceases with the stimulation of VMH satiety centre by blood glucose level rising above a set point. The action of the satiety centre is to inhibit the feeding centre.

However, there are problems with this theory. Closer examination of the behaviour of animals following VMH lesions reveals that the result is not simply endless hyperphagia (see Figure 5.1). Usually, the huge increase in food intake for 12 days or so is followed by recovery to an asymptotic value. After this weight is maintained at a new, higher level, but food intake is only slightly higher than normal. If the rat is starved at this stage, its weight falls, but when the animal is again given free access to food, it

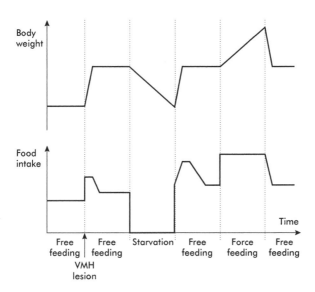

FIGURE 5.1 Food intake and body weight of rats with various manipulations after lesions in the ventromedial hypothalamus

eats large quantities until its weight again stabilises at the higher level. Conversely, force-feeding is followed by a reduction of eating, again until the weight is re-stabilised. Interestingly, these results depend on the animals being provided with a diet that is not only nutritious but also palatable. If the palatability of the food available to the animals is low, then the hyperphagia is less, and the asymptotic weight is not much higher than that of unoperated animals (Sclafani, Springer and Kluge, 1976). So, VMH lesions do not prevent the control of food intake, they seem to cause the set point for body weight to be increased. This seems to be the result of damage caused by VMH lesions to pathways that mediate PNS control over the secretion of the pancreatic hormones. This has two effects: it increases insulin production so that more energy is stored in the form of body fat, and it decreases glucagon secretion, making the stored energy less accessible (Kirchgessner and Sclafani, 1988).

It also became apparent that lesions in, and stimulation of, the LH produce not only changes in eating, but also in drinking, as we saw in Chapter 4. Furthermore, Teitelbaum and Stellar (1954) showed that most LH-lesioned rats would start to eat and drink again, as long as they were kept alive long enough by being given food and water through a tube into the stomach. Just as VMH-lesioned rats stabilise their weight at a new, higher level, so LH-lesioned rats maintain their weight at a lower level. Force-feeding and starving, and changes in palatability of food, all have exactly parallel effects in lesioned rats and controls. So, although it is clearly true that centres in the VMH and the LH exert control over eating, there must be other control mechanisms that can take over their functions if necessary, and may indeed act in parallel with them.

The gastrointestinal tract

Doubts about the dual-centre set-point theory led in the 1970s and 1980s to new experimental work on the role of the gastrointestinal tract. It had long been known that the stomach can provide a satiety signal, since injection of food directly into the stomach of hungry experimental animals stops them eating. **Sham feeding**, in which animals are given fistulas preventing food from reaching their stomachs, results in copious eating. This sham eating is stopped by injections of food directly into the stomach. Conversely, removal of food from the stomach starts an animal eating again (Davis and Campbell, 1973). At first it was thought that this indicated either that nutrients absorbed into the blood from the intestines triggered satiety (consistent with glucostatic theories), or that there is some direct sensory signal (perhaps stretch receptors in the stomach) that have this effect. However, these cannot be the only mechanisms. First, preventing the passage of food from the stomach does not stop the satiety mechanism (Deutsch and Gonzalez, 1980); second, the pressure in the stomach does not increase following eating (Young and Deutsch, 1980); and third, denervation of the stomach does not prevent the cessation of feeding (Gonzalez and Deutsch, 1981).

Multiple controls

In the past 15–20 years it has come to be recognised that the physiological mechanisms for the control of eating are multiple and redundant (Bernardis and Bellinger, 1996). It is beyond the scope of this book to try to detail these complexities and, in any case, the pace of research is such that a summary would be soon out of date. I will simply describe some of the systems that are being investigated currently, without attempting to suggest how they interact to control eating.

Peptides (chains of amino acids smaller than proteins) are produced by endocrine cells in the lining of the stomach and intestines in response to food. These peptides include **cholecysto-kinin (CCK)**, insulin and *bombesin*, although there are probably others. These peptides have both peripheral and central actions producing satiety. Peripheral injection of CCK into rats and humans causes them to stop eating (Smith and Gibbs, 1994). This peripheral effect of CCK is mediated by the autonomic afferents in the **vagus nerve** (Guan, Phillips and Green, 1996). Bombesin also has peripheral action. Its effect is not reduced by cutting the vagus but is by total separation of the gut from the CNS, suggesting that it acts as a satiety signal from lower in the tract. Peptides (e.g. *amylin)* are also secreted by the pancreas in response to food. These also act by stimulating afferent fibres from the gut (Lutz *et al.*, 1998), as well as having direct actions in the CNS. Woods *et al.* (1996) have shown that pancreatic insulin crosses the blood–brain barrier, and attaches to receptors in the hypothalamus. However, Chapman *et al.* (1998) have shown that, in the levels actually found in the body, insulin has no effect in the short term on hunger or food intake in humans, and that its long-term effects are likely to be secondary to its metabolic effect on glucose. The autonomic afferents from the gut enter the CNS in, amongst other places, the NST and the PBN. High concentrations of CCK and other peptides are found in these locations where they seem to act as neurotransmitters. The NST also receives inputs from sensory systems in the mouth and has axons extending to the VMH.

Peptides are also involved in the *commencement* of feeding. **Neuropeptide Y** (NPY) is found in many parts of the brain, especially in the paraventricular nucleus (PVN) and other parts of the hypothalamus, and in brain stem areas such as the NST and the PBN. Injection of NPY into the hypothalamus causes sated rats to start feeding (Clark *et al.*, 1984). However, the role of this is not clear. Pedrazzi *et al.* (1998) have shown that rats that become obese after being given free access to a varied and highly palatable diet have increased NPY in the PVN at an early stage in their weight gain, but that this subsequently returns to normal while weight gain continues. Rats that did not become obese under the same regime showed normal NPY, but increased amounts of another peptide, *galanin*, in the arcuate nucleus. The arcuate nucleus sends fibres to the PVN, probably using galanin as neurotransmitter.

The physiological control of weight therefore seems to be a complex interaction of neurotransmitters, hormones, peripheral chemical and sensory factors, and brain nuclei. In addition, as suggested by the longer-term consequences of VMH lesions that we looked at earlier, it is clear that there are separate, but related, control systems for the control of meal size and of body weight. The complexity of this is indicated further by experiments on a strain of rats, *Zucker rats*, which carry a gene that causes hyperphagia and obesity. Cole, Berman, and Bodner (1997) have pointed out that systems based on opioids, norepinephrine, dopamine, NPY, 5-HT, histamine, galanin and CCK have all been shown to be involved in the production of obesity in these animals.

Psychological influences on eating

The enormous complexity of the control of eating seen in the physiological mechanisms is further increased by a consideration of other influences, which we turn to next.

Palatability

The first, obvious factor is the palatability of food. Humans, and other animals, will eat more readily, and also will eat more food, when the food tastes nice than if it is rendered less palatable, for example by the addition of quinine. Even rats made hyperphagic by VMH lesions eat less unpalatable food, and stabilise at a lower weight. To use the same jargon as for drinking, food has *positive incentive value*, and more palatable food has a higher incentive value. Conversely, under conditions of deprivation palatability increases (Cabanac, 1979). Capaldi (1996a) has pointed out that this palatability does not extend equally across different foods or tastes. Specifically, anecdotal evidence suggests that under extreme deprivation preference for, and palatability of, sweet foods declines, while that of savoury foods increases. The administration of opioid antagonists reduces pleasantness ratings of foods, and Le Magnen (1990) suggested that the rewarding properties of eating are due to the release of endogenous opioids in the hypothalamus.

Sensory-specific satiety

Eating a particular food has several related consequences. During its consumption, the rate of eating slows, and this is followed for up to an hour by a decrease in rated palatability, and by a decreased likelihood that the same food will be chosen again when one is offered a choice. These effects are all specific to the particular food eaten, and are known as **sensory-specific satiety** (see Hetherington and Rolls, 1996). This can be observed during a meal: even when you have eaten enough of the main course to feel completely sated, and may be unable to finish the dish, you might yet 'find room' for a dessert, even though that dessert may contain more calories and carbohydrate than you have already eaten.

In experiments with rats (see Swithers and Hall, 1994) it has been shown that sensory-specific satiety occurs in sham-feeding animals. It does not, therefore, depend on post-ingestive factors; that is, no nutrients need to be absorbed. Further, it clearly occurs in response to the flavour of food, and is independent of its nutritive properties. It must, therefore, be based on the sensory properties of foods. The only macronutrients that are detectable by taste are the sugars; the apparently distinctive flavours of fats and proteins come from molecules associated with them in foods. Of the other nutrients, only salt is associated with a specific gustatory sensation. Nevertheless, the adaptive function of sensory-specific satiety is presumably to facilitate variety in diet. Since flavour and nutrient composition are generally correlated in foods, sensory-specific satiety provides a mechanism that will, within limits, ensure variety of nutritional intake.

Sensory-specific satiety is an example of the process of *non-associative learning* known as **habituation**. Repeated or continued presentation of the same stimulus results in a decreased behavioural and physiological response to that stimulus, but the response returns when the stimulus is altered. Rolls (1993) demonstrated that cells in the LH originally thought to be responsive to food are actually responsive to incentive properties of food, and are involved in, or at least reflect, the process of sensory-specific satiety. That is, although their activity declines in the presence of food that has just been eaten, they remain active to different food, to the sight of different food and to stimuli conditioned to food.

Learning what to eat

Newborn infants show distinctive facial responses to sweet, sour, bitter and possibly salt stimuli placed in the mouth. The responses to sour and bitter tastes involve expulsive mouth movements. Newborns also show taste preferences, shown by faster sucking rates and/or higher food intake when offered sweet liquids to drink. Most studies of the gustatory responses of newborns show no specific response to salt, and in preference tests infants seem to be indifferent to salty tastes. There is good evidence for aversive responses to sour liquids, and some for aversive response to strongly bitter tastes (see Mennella and Beauchamp, 1996). It has been argued that these have evolved to protect against eating substances that may be injurious; many poisons have a bitter taste.

Similarly, it has been argued that the pleasantness of sweet tastes indicates foods that may be good to eat. Beyond this (and partly on the basis of this) animals (and people) learn which foods are good to eat and which are not. One example of this is the development of preference for salty tastes during the first six months of life (Harris and Booth, 1987).

Although there is some evidence for prenatal influences on food preference in other species, in humans the learning of taste preferences starts soon after birth. Early deficits of sodium have been shown to lead to a greater salt appetite when the children are older (Beauchamp and Cowart, 1993). Flavours of foods eaten by a mother are transferred to her milk, and in animal and human research have been shown to influence the offspring's food preferences (see Mennella and Beauchamp, 1996). This can be interpreted as a way in which young mammals learn which foods are good to eat.

Principles of associative learning provide the most powerful source of food preferences. I shall consider two main ways, apart from the mere exposure mentioned above, in which we learn food preferences (see Capaldi, 1996a). *Flavour–flavour learning* results from the association of a new flavour with one that is already preferred. The most obvious example of this is the association of flavours with sweetness that is innately preferred and this has been demonstrated in numerous animal and human experiments. In one study of humans, for example (Zellner *et al.*, 1983), subjects expressed a preference for unfamiliar varieties of tea that were sweetened over those that were not. This preference continued even when the teas were subsequently tried unsweetened, demonstrating that the preference had been learned by the association of the flavour of the tea with the previously preferred sweetness.

The second principle of learning is *flavour–nutrient learning* when a new preference is established by pairing a flavour with some other food that has nutritive properties. This was shown in rats, for example, by Sclafani and Nissenbaum (1988). They gave rats water with one of two different flavours, and arranged that each time they took a drink from one particular flavour, a nutritious solution was delivered directly to the stomach. After four days the animals, when given a choice between the two flavours, chose the one which had previously been associated with the nutritious results. Thus, these animals had learned which taste indicated the supply of nutritious food.

I should mention one further, very important, source of learning on diet that has received less research attention, and that is direct parental influence. The foods that we find most palatable without learning are sweet foods, while 'healthy' foods are less palatable. The adoption of a healthy diet, therefore, must be based on learning, and much of this learning takes place within the family. Birch and Fisher (1996) have pointed out that within the family, the eating of these less palatable foods is more often associated with negative affect (coercion, threats or actual punishment) than with positive affect, while inherently palatable foods, high in carbohydrates often combined with fats, are presented in pleasant contexts (parties, treats, etc.). This makes it difficult for the child to learn healthy eating habits, particularly as it is combined with *neophobia*; a distrust of trying new foods, that is common in children and in other species, presumably as a protective device.

Learning what not to eat

We also learn what *not* to eat through a process known as **conditioned aversion** (or *taste aversion learning*; see Schafe and Bernstein, 1996). In an early study, for example, Garcia and Koelling (1966) gave rats saccharine to taste then injected them with a lithium salt, which causes distress (interpreted as nausea, which lithium induces in humans). After just one such experience the rats learned not to drink saccharine solutions. Rats given electric shocks in association with saccharine did *not* learn to avoid saccharine. Aversion can be conditioned to particular tastes, or to the smell, sight or even thought of particular foods. Many people develop an aversion to foods that have made them ill, or have otherwise been associated with ill effects. The significance of conditioned aversion, of course, is that a food that has once made an animal ill is likely to do so again and so must be avoided.

Conditioned aversion has some similarities to standard classical (Pavlovian) conditioning. The aversive response shows *generalisation* to similar tastes, with the response declining the more different the tastes are from the conditioned one. The aversive response shows *extinction* after repeated, non-reinforced presentations of the original food. However, it also shows important differences from classical conditioning. The response is formed in a single trial, which is very unusual for classical conditioning, in which a response becomes associated with the conditional stimulus only gradually. Conditioned aversion can also take place when the food and the sickness are separated by a relatively long interval, of up to 12 hours. In classical conditioning delays of only a few seconds usually prevent the formation of conditioned responses. These differences not only made the learning theorists of the 1960s reluctant to accept Garcia's results, but are crucial if conditioned aversion is to have its protective effect. An animal could not learn to avoid poisonous food over a number of pairings of food and sickness; the learning *needs* to take place in one trial. Similarly, the ill-effects of poisonous food are frequently delayed by hours.

Conditioned aversion is usually considered to be based on a different mechanism to classical conditioning. Garcia, Hankins and Rusiniak (1974) have suggested that it is based on simple neural circuits in the NST and the PBN which, as we have seen, are the sites of convergence of visceral and taste afferents. However, it has been shown that decerebrate rats (animals with the cerebral hemispheres removed) are unable to form conditioned aversion (Grill and Norgren, 1978), so that the involvement of the neocortex seems to be necessary.

Learning when to eat

We also learn *when* to eat. Human beings tend to eat at fixed times of day. Rats can learn quickly to associate regular times of day with feeding and secrete insulin in anticipation at those times of day (see Woods, 1995). Rats which have been conditioned to associate the availability of food with an audible stimulus will subsequently eat more when those stimuli are repeated, even when food is continuously available between stimuli (Weingarten, 1983). Humans kept in isolation from the normal cues to the time of day (see Chapter 3) often change their eating patterns to fewer, larger meals (Bernstein, 1981). Thus, eating (or hunger) is triggered by internal circadian rhythms and external stimuli associated with daily activity cycles, as well as by specific stimuli like the sound of crockery and cutlery.

Clearly, we may conclude from all of the foregoing that not only are the physiological control processes multiple, but that they interact with, and can be overridden by, various learned and other psychological factors. One extreme demonstration of the human being's ability to override physiological hunger mechanisms is the fact that it is possible for people voluntarily to starve themselves to death, for example in the process of a hunger strike. In the following sections we will look at other examples of the human ability to escape from the constraints of physiological mechanisms.

Disorders of eating and weight control

Obesity

Whether or not we describe somebody as obese depends on the reason for providing a label. In general, the term *obesity* may be used simply to refer to having more than average body fat. Despite recent doubts about the quality and consistency of some of the research on which the conclusion is based, it is generally accepted that a high level of obesity, *medically significant obesity*, is injurious to health, contributing to a wide range of morbid conditions, especially cardiovascular disease (Rand, 1994). Aside from this, obesity may be *culturally defined*, that is, a person may be described as obese if he or she has more body fat than is considered aesthetically acceptable by the person's society. In this section, I will not be concerned with such distinctions, but will look at the factors that cause variations in body fat between individuals, and will use the general definition given above, of having more than average body fat.

Obesity results only from taking in more calories than we expend. However, beyond this simple relation is a large number of potential reasons for the existence of such an imbalance. One obvious factor, as we have seen, is the easy availability of processed foods of high palatability in western societies. This clearly can increase calorie consumption and may change the set point so that body weight stabilises at a higher level. But this cannot be the sole explanation. Not everybody exposed to such a potential diet becomes obese, and obesity has a higher incidence in some developed countries (USA and UK, for example) than in others, even if the others actually have a higher average calorie consumption (e.g. Denmark).

One undoubted factor is learning. Children in many families are encouraged or even forced to eat all the food placed in front of them. This can lead to eating more calories than required and can become an habitual pattern. This is exacerbated by the division of meals into more than one course, with the opportunity this provides for sensory-specific satiety to increase total calorie intake, particularly if the meal pattern reserves energy-dense foods until the end of the meal. Energy-dense foods, that is foods with a high concentration of calories per unit weight, usually fat-based foods, are highly rewarding, particularly if they are sweet. The association of sweetness with high-fat content of many processed foods is, as we saw earlier, the basis for a learned preference for these foods. Many obese people, and others who indulge in binge eating, show a preference, and often a craving, for such high-density foods, but not, the most recent research suggests, for low-fat sweet foods (see Drewnowski, 1996). Drewnowski et al. (1995) have shown by the use of opiate receptor blockers that this preference is based on endogenous **opioid** circuits (presumably beta-endorphins). This can account for phenomena related to 'comfort-eating' when food is used to elevate mood, and may permit us to talk about food addictions (see Chapter 8).

There is certainly a genetic factor involved in weight control as well. Stunkard et al. (1986) showed that the weight of people who had been adopted in infancy is more highly correlated with the weight of their natural parents than with that of their adoptive parents. Strains of mice and rats have been bred with a genetic predisposition to obesity. Although these particular strains of rodent develop obesity even on standard laboratory diets, other strains show individual differences in their predisposition to obesity which are only manifest if they are given high calorie and/or varied diets. The genetic basis of human obesity is likely to be of this latter type, depending on the individual being exposed to particular family, social and cultural environments. People clearly differ in metabolic efficiency, and most people respond to excessive calorie intake in a different way from very obese persons. In one study, Sims and Horton (1968) gave normal weight prisoners varied, highly palatable, high calorie meals several times each day. All subjects increased their calorie intake enormously, with some eating more than twice the average amount for sedentary people. Despite this, they only gained a small amount of weight, and at the end of experiment they returned to their usual diets and their previous weights.

It is partly because of the hereditary contribution that obesity, with its implications for health, is difficult to treat. Whatever method is used, ranging from calorie-reduced diets to surgical removal of fat and reduction of the size of the stomach, weight loss is rarely maintained in the long term. Another factor maintaining obesity has been called the 'yo-yo' effect. This is the increased metabolic efficiency that occurs after severe calorie restriction, and has been demonstrated in laboratory animals and in humans. In one such study Brownell *et al.* (1986) fed rats a high calorie, palatable diet until they became obese. On average it took 46 days for the rats to reach the criterion of obesity. The animals were then starved until their weights returned to normal and were then again fed the high calorie diet. This time it took only 14 days for the rats to become obese. The implication is that their metabolic efficiency had increased so that more energy was stored as fat. This same process may take place in people who lose weight by calorie restriction, making it harder for them to avoid putting weight on again.

Anorexia nervosa

The name **anorexia nervosa** is usually inappropriate since it literally means absence of appetite. Most sufferers actually have a desire for (even a great interest in) food. Marx (1994) has summarised the enormous number and range of theories for the aetiology of anorexia nervosa. These have ranged from the discredited proposal earlier this century that it results from underactivity of the anterior pituitary gland, through the psychodynamic theories that predominated in the middle decades of this century, to more recent approaches that suggest a multiplicity of social, family and personal factors that predispose the individual, precipitate the illness and perpetuate its course.

Many studies have reported that particular physiological changes or abnormalities are present in anorexic persons. To take two recent examples, Fujimoto *et al.* (1997) reported that restrictive (low weight) anorexics, but not binge-purging anorexics, showed an increased CCK and pancreatic peptide response to a fat-rich meal. Gordon, Lask and Bryant-Waugh (1997), arguing for a multifactorial aetiology of anorexia, including a biological substrate, have demonstrated that a group of anorexic children had reduced blood flow in one temporal lobe of the cerebral cortex, and that this persisted in three children who recovered and returned to normal weight. The problem with these sorts of findings is, first, that such changes might be a result of, rather than a cause of the profound physiological consequences of anorexia. Second, eating disorders are undoubtedly multifactorial, and the complexity and redundancy that we have seen in the physiological mechanisms underlying normal food intake make it unlikely that a disorder in any one component would have such a profound effect.

An alternative view is that it might be sensible to consider anorexia not primarily as an eating disorder but rather as a manifestation of other problems. This is reflected in the predominance of psychological and socio-cultural factors in theories of the aetiology of anorexia (and other eating disorders). From this point of view, the main interest of anorexia for the purpose of this chapter is that it illustrates the power of such non-physiological factors to override the physiological mechanisms I have described.

Bulimia nervosa

The main characteristic of bulimia is binge eating. Binge eating may occur without other behaviours or problems, and will then result in obesity. It may also occur with vomiting or purging, and that may either allow the maintenance of an average ('normal') body weight, or be associated with the maintenance of a low body weight. As I noted earlier, bingeing often concentrates on foods with a high energy density. As with anorexia, the processes reflect control over eating by psychological factors rather than by physiological ones. The causative and maintaining factors may again be varied and complex and most workers recognise the importance of interacting social and psychological factors. Also as with anorexia, it is not useful to view bulimia as primarily a problem of control of hunger and eating, and I shall not consider it further here.

Summary

Food provides energy and specific nutritive components, some of which cannot be synthesised by the body. Most energy is stored between meals in the form of fats. The storage and release of this energy is controlled by the hormones insulin and glucagon. Simple theories about the control of hunger and food intake proposed that they are based on gastric contractions, or glucostatic mechanisms, the last operating through a feeding centre in the lateral hypothalamus and a satiety centre in the ventromedial hypothalamus (the dual-centre set-point theory). Many difficulties with this approach led to a reconsideration of the gastrointestinal tract as a source of hunger and satiety. The current view of the control of eating is that there are multiple parallel systems based in several peripheral and central structures, and based on numerous hormones and neurotransmitters. Of enormous importance for human eating are psychological factors, including palatability and learning. It is clearly established that a major component of our eating, and that of other species, results from learning what to eat and what not to eat, and when to eat. This learning is based on habituation (sensory-specific satiety), on associative learning (particularly flavour–flavour learning and conditioned aversion), and on simple exposure and parental control. Underlying all of these processes is an innate preference for sweet-tasting foods. Obesity and eating disorders are multifactorial conditions. Obesity depends on an interaction between genetic and socio-cultural factors. Anorexia and bulimia nervosa are best not considered as primary disorders of the control of eating, but, like hunger strikes, illustrate the human capacity to override physiological constraints on eating.

Further reading

Bray, G. A., Bouchard, C. and Jones, P. T. (1997) *The Handbook of Obesity*, New York: Marcel Dekker. Includes a useful overview of the neuroscience of eating and weight control by S. F. Leibowitz and B. G. Hoebel.

Brownell, K. D. (1997) *Handbook of Obesity and Eating Disorders*, New York: Basic Books. The new edition of this standard work which is recognised as an authoritative review of disorders of eating.

Capaldi, E. D. (ed.) (1996) *Why We Eat What We Eat: The Psychology of Eating*. Washington, DC: American Psychological Association. This volume concentrates on the role of learning and socio-cultural factors in eating. The chapters are written by some of the leading authorities in the field.

Szmukler, G., Dare, C. and Treasure, J. (eds) (1995) *Handbook of Eating Disorders: Theory, Treatment and Research*, Chichester: Wiley. In this volume leading authors describe the history, consequences, treatment, prevention and theories of the aetiology of eating disorders.

Chapter 6

Sex

THE ENHANCEMENT OF THE proportion of one's own genes in the next generation may be considered the prime underlying motivating force of all organisms. In no field of motivation is this more directly expressed than in sex. Most mammals show a reproductive pattern, known as promiscuity, in which most females mate with several males and most males never mate. Those dominant males who do mate do so with several females. Human mating systems are less easy to define so simply because they show much greater variability. The predominant mammalian pattern of promiscuity is frowned upon in most human societies, the majority of which are described as monogamous denoting that a male and female form an exclusive pair. Humans are unusual in this respect as monogamy is relatively rare in mammalian species. Human monogamy may be serial, meaning that partners may be changed.

Humans are unusual, also, in that our sexual behaviour is much less stereotypical than that of the animals most studied to investigate neural and endocrine systems involved in sexual behaviour. Furthermore, we are much less driven by biological factors than are other species, despite the efforts of sociobiologists to explain human sexual behaviour in terms of adaptive features noted in other species. In sex, as in all of the other topics we cover in this book, much of the information we use comes from animal studies. The problem of extrapolating from these findings to humans is particularly obvious in relation to sex, and is apparent in these very different mating patterns, the variability of human sexual behaviour, and the control we are able to exercise over our own behaviour.

In this chapter we will be particularly concerned with endocrine influences on sex and sexual behaviour. We start by examining briefly the origin of the structural differences between males and females.

Sexual differentiation

Clearly, men and women usually look different. Some of the differences, such as in the external genitalia, are apparent at birth, and some are there but cannot be seen (the internal genital organs). Other differences appear at puberty (the secondary sex characteristics). All of these structural differences, and behavioural differences, are together called **sexual dimorphism**.

Males and females are usually differentiated genetically by the fact that females possess two X chromosomes, while males possess one X and one Y chromosome. Up to about six weeks after fertilisation, male and female human embryos are otherwise identical. The sexual dimorphism of humans stems almost entirely from a gene on the Y chromosome, which at six weeks produces a protein, the **HY antigen**, which starts a chain of biochemical events resulting in the undifferentiated gonads of male embryos developing into testes (see Figure 6.1). The testes then produce

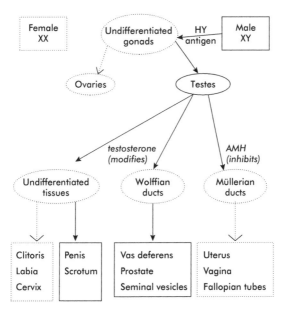

FIGURE 6.1 The effect of testicular hormones on sexual differentiation

two substances, the androgen hormone testosterone, and anti-Müllerian hormone (AMH; also known as Müllerian-inhibiting substance). Testosterone causes the male embryo to develop the male genitalia (seminal vesicles, vas deferens, scrotum, penis, etc.) from the **Wolffian ducts** and other tissues, while AMH prevents the development of the female internal genitalia from the **Müllerian ducts**. In the female, the *absence* of these substances allows the development of female genitalia (uterus, fallopian tubes, labia, clitoris, etc.), while the Müllerian ducts atrophy.

While sexual differentiation in the embryo depends almost entirely on the presence or absence of testosterone, changes at puberty are mostly produced by what I shall call 'sex-appropriate' hormones; that is, androgens in males and oestrogens in females. Testosterone leads to the secondary sex characteristics of the male adult body (beard growth, increased muscle bulk, growth of external genitalia, enlargement of vocal cords and larynx), while oestrogens from the ovaries produce the female changes (breast development, subcutaneous fat deposits, onset of menstruation). The exception to this is that the growth of pubic and axillary hair in both sexes results from androgens (in females, secreted mainly by the adrenal cortices).

Such effects of hormones, producing changes preparing the body for particular functions, are known as **organising effects**. However, not all such organising effects are so clearly structural, and we will look at behavioural organising effects on pp. 94–6.

Activating effects of sex hormones

Rats, and other species studied in the laboratory, have highly stereotyped (species-typical) patterns of sexual activity, and these are clearly differentiated between the sexes. To simplify things, female rats show stereotyped **proceptive behaviours**, which include running towards and away from the male in a particular manner. However, she only does this when progesterone levels are high, at the appropriate phase of the oestrus cycle. The effect of this on the male is to cause him to stay near the female, usually sniffing her.

The male rat will try to mount the female. In response to the tactile stimulation on her flanks, the female's proceptive behaviours are replaced by **receptive behaviour**, characterised by a particular stance called **lordosis**, which permits copulation to occur.

The occurrence of these stereotyped behaviours depends on the presence of sex-appropriate hormones. The behaviours are completely abolished within days by removal of the gonads of adult animals, and are reinstated immediately by the injection of sex-appropriate hormones. Injection of sex-*inappropriate* hormones has little or no effect. In animals that have annual breeding cycles, testosterone production almost stops during parts of the year when breeding does not take place. This type of hormone effect is called an **activating effect**, since the hormone causes the activation of programmed behaviours.

Activating effects in males

Male rodents show wide individual differences in sexual activity, but these individual differences are not related to adult testosterone levels. If castration, leading to cessation of sexual activity, is followed by testosterone injection, so that sexual activity is reinstated, the amount of sexual activity does not depend on the amount of injected hormone. Instead, the original individual differences re-occur. What is more, reduction of the amount of testosterone to only one-tenth of the level before castration is enough to reinstate previous levels of sexual activity. Giving more testosterone does not increase sexual activity (Grunt and Young, 1953).

So, testosterone acts with a threshold effect: once the animal has a certain, critical level, it can, and will, engage in sexual activity given the appropriate external stimuli. This is described as a *permissive* effect; a certain level of a hormone permits a particular behaviour to take place, but the actual occurrence of that behaviour depends on other factors. The presence of a female animal in the receptive stage of the oestrus cycle produces a measurable increase in the male's testosterone level. So, sexual behaviour of a male rodent depends on the co-occurrence of external factors (a proceptive and receptive female conspecific) and of internal factors (the perinatal and developmental organising effects of testosterone, together with the current activating effects of circulating hormones). These external and internal factors are interrelated, in that the male animal's behaviour helps to stimulate relevant behaviour in the female, while her behaviour stimulates both sexual behaviour and hormonal changes in the male.

Men are rather like rats, at least where the effects of testosterone are concerned. Castration of adult men leads in most cases to a reduction or cessation of sexual activity. But, whereas in rats this is usually complete and occurs within a few weeks, in men the effect is much more variable. Bremer (1959) studied 157 Norwegian men who had been castrated, mostly in return for a reduction of prison sentences after conviction for sexual crimes. Seventy-four of the men, like rats, became effectively asexual within a few weeks of the operation and another twenty-nine did so within a year. Most of the others lost their ability to achieve erections within a year, but many continued to report sexual interest. A few remained sexually active. Later studies, using both surgical and 'chemical' castration (administration of a substance that blocks androgen receptors), have suggested that a somewhat higher proportion remain sexually active.

Testosterone levels in men also *respond* to sexual behaviour: viewing erotic films increases blood testosterone levels (Hellhammer, Hubert and Schurmeyer, 1985). However, in intact men most research finds no relationship between the *level* of testosterone and the intensity of sexual desire or amount of sexual activity (just as in rats). Once we have an above-threshold amount more testosterone does not increase desire or performance. One or two more recent studies have, however, found a relation between testosterone level above the threshold and sexual activity (Alexander *et al.*, 1997).

Activating effects in females

Female animals in many species are as active in initiating copulation as are males. Their readiness to engage in proceptive and receptive behaviour depends on cyclic release of gonadal hormones (the oestrus cycle). In rats, for example, this cycle is four days, with circulating levels of the oestrogen oestradiol peaking some 40 hours before the female becomes receptive. Immediately before the receptive period progesterone is secreted coinciding with ovulation. So, sexual behaviour in mammals other than primates is virtually restricted to the most fertile phase of the cycle. The consequences of ovariectomy (surgical removal of the ovaries) in female rats and guinea pigs are quick and highly consistent; there is a rapid decline into complete absence of sexual behaviour. The reinstatement of full proceptive and receptive behaviour in ovariectomised rats by hormone replacement requires matching the natural sequence of hormone production. If this is done the reinstatement is rapid and complete (Takahashi, 1990).

The relation between women's sexual behaviour and hormones is much less like that in rats than is that of men. The menstrual cycle is a cycle of hormonal changes, including the sequential secretion of oestradiol and progesterone that I mentioned in rats. In humans levels of oestradiol peak at around the time of ovulation and progesterone peaks a few days later (see Figure 2.5). Although this pattern is somewhat later in the cycle than it is in rats, the hormonal sequence suggests that sexual interest and behaviour should be greatest at the most fertile time during the cycle. Most research has shown that women experience their highest level of sexual desire or activity immediately after menstruation, when conception is least likely (see McNeill, 1994). Such a pattern might result from abstinence during menstruation, but the important point is that it suggests that there is no relation between sexual arousability, desire or activity and levels of circulating hormones. However, it might be important to distinguish, as Baker and Bellis (1995) do, amongst sexual activity with different immediate aims, which most of this research has not done. For example, Bellis and Baker (1990) demonstrated that women are more likely to have sex with somebody other than their usual partner (extra-pair copulations) during the most fertile part of the cycle, but with their usual partner during the least fertile period.

The lack of close relation between women's sexual behaviour and female hormones is also shown by the effects of ovariectomy in adult women, and of the loss of female hormones after the menopause, neither of which directly affects sexual interest nor necessarily behaviour. It is now widely accepted that women's sexual drive is more closely affected by androgens (secreted by the adrenal cortex and the ovaries) than by oestrogens. This is shown by several lines of evidence. First, correlational studies in healthy women have shown a relation between sexual interest and testosterone (Alexander and Sherwin, 1993). Second, some studies have shown that higher testosterone levels are associated with higher frequency of masturbation in women (e.g. Bancroft et al., 1991). Third, testosterone injections have been shown to increase sexual interest in women after hysterectomy (which also removes the ovaries) and after the menopause, but oestradiol injections have no effect (e.g. Sherwin and Gelfand, 1987). Fourth, the commencement of sexual intercourse at puberty for young women is correlated with the rise in testosterone levels at that time (Halpern, Udry and Suchindran, 1997). Furthermore, circulating testosterone peaks during the most fertile phase of the menstrual cycle (van Goozen et al., 1997).

Organising effects of testosterone

The development of male or female sexual behaviour depends on the perinatal presence or absence of androgens. The experiments on which this conclusion is based have mostly involved injecting pregnant rodents with hormones and testing for their effects on the offspring. If testosterone is injected into a pregnant guinea pig, and her female offspring are tested by removal of the ovaries and subsequent replacement of hormones, then the female offspring show a masculine response to injections of androgens (Phoenix et al., 1959). That is, these female guinea pigs will attempt to mount other females. This is called a **masculinising effect**. Further, they do not show the normal proceptive and receptive responses to oestrogen injections. This is a **defeminising effect**. The reverse pattern is shown in male animals. Here, the manipulation is to *prevent* testosterone exposure by castrating the rats at birth. Later hormone trials show a **feminising effect**, in which the male rats respond with female patterns of behaviour to oestrogen injections, and a **demasculinising effect**, in which injection of testosterone into the adult male rats does not produce the usual male mounting and copulatory behaviour in the presence of a receptive female.

This sort of experiment clearly demonstrates that perinatal testosterone levels have sex-specific organising effects on rodents. Most evidence points to this being an effect on brain structures which we will look at later. Do these sorts of results have implications for human sexual behaviour? Such results have sometimes been used as an explanation for human homosexuality, and I will look at this sort of argument later. But what *are* the effects of increased or decreased perinatal androgen levels in humans? The experiments on rats cannot, of course, be carried out on people, but two pathological conditions occur which have similar effects.

Androgen insensitivity syndrome occurs in persons who are genetically male, have testes that produce testosterone and AMH, but who have no androgen receptors. The AMH inhibits the development of female internal genitalia, while the effective absence of testosterone prevents male internal and external genitalia developing. They are born with normal female external genitalia and are generally raised as girls. At puberty the body responds to the small amounts of oestrogens produced in the adrenal cortex and what appear to be normal female changes (apart from the menstrual cycle) occur. These people generally think of themselves as women and generally show the usual female sexual preferences and behaviour. This could be interpreted as feminisation and demasculinisation of genetic males in the effective absence of perinatal testosterone (see Money and Ehrhardt, 1972). However, note that the feminine behaviour of these people could equally result from them being treated as female all their lives.

Adrenogenital syndrome (or congenital adrenal hyperplasia) occurs in both genetic males and genetic females in whom, as a result of a variety of genetic errors, the adrenal cortex secretes unusually high amounts of androgens. In genetic females the effect is variable, depending on how much androgen is produced, and results in varying degrees of masculinisation of the external genitalia, often giving an indeterminate appearance of gender. Before the cause and treatment of these cases was worked out in around 1950, these genetically female children were raised as either boys or girls depending, presumably, on the form of the genitalia and the inclination of the parents. At puberty there was no problem for those assigned to the female gender as a normal female puberty ensued. However, for those raised as boys, the female puberty was inconsistent with their assigned gender, which frequently caused serious distress. Several studies have shown that genetic females with adrenogenital syndrome are more likely to choose female sexual partners than are the rest of the female population (e.g. Dittman, Kappes and Kappes, 1992). This is true even of those given surgery immediately after birth and treated for the hormone imbalance. However, these are unusual people who are aware of their condition and have to take medication constantly. The outcome might result from altered self-perception and/or treatment by other people.

Brain mechanisms

An area of the forebrain just in front of the hypothalamus, the medial preoptic area (MPA), has long been known to be essential for sexual behaviour in male laboratory animals. Destruction of this area in a wide range of species permanently stops them engaging in sexual activity (e.g. Heimer and Larsson, 1966/7). Conversely, electrical stimulation of this region produces mounting behaviour in male rats (Malsbury, 1972), and activity of the cells there increases during normal copulation (Mas, 1995). Lesions in the MPA do not prevent the animals showing sexual interest, nor do they prevent erection in response to manual stimulation. Operated male rats will show preparatory behaviours (pursuit and sniffing of a female), and operated male monkeys will masturbate and show interest in a female. However, in neither case will they mount the female.

In 1978, Gorski and his colleagues demonstrated that the MPA has a nucleus that is three to five times larger in male rats than in female rats. This region became known as the **sexually** dimorphic nucleus (SDN) of the preoptic area. Such a difference has also been found in humans. Castration immediately after birth prevents the SDN from retaining its greater size in males, so this sexual dimorphism of the CNS is the result of an organising effect of perinatal androgens (Rhees, Shryne and Gorski, 1990). Castration of adult animals causes some areas within the SDN to shrink (Bloch and Gorski, 1988) suggesting that this is the locus of action of at least some of the activating effects of testosterone. The MPA controls the cyclical or constant rates of secretion of hormones that are typical of females and males, respectively. A number of other sexually dimorphic areas have been found in the CNS. These include the **third interstitial nucleus of the anterior hypothalamus (INAH-3)**, which we will look at in a later section; the bed nucleus of the stria terminalis (BNST; the stria terminalis is a tract that connects the amygdala to the MPA), which is larger in men than in women; and an area in the spinal cord that is involved in penile erection. Rodents also show sex differences in the size of two fibre bundles that join the two cerebral hemispheres, the corpus callosum and the **anterior commissure**. Recent reviews have cast doubt on earlier claims that the same differences occur in humans, in whom they had been used to explain some sex differences in cognition (Bishop and Wahlstein, 1997; Noonan *et al.*, 1998).

Males

In recent years enormous advances have been made in the study of the neural systems involved in the sexual behaviour of rodents. Wood (1997) has summarised the systems in male hamsters as a three-dimensional model, the details of which are beyond the scope of this chapter. The neural networks that she describes serve to integrate sensory information (including olfactory and pheromonal inputs from the olfactory bulbs) and internal hormonal factors (through receptors in a sub-circuit involving the *medial amygdala* and the MPA). The MPA is connected to midbrain areas that seem to organise the motor control of sexual activity. The major centres and influences are summarised in Figure 6.2.

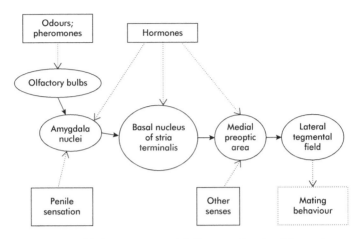

FIGURE 6.2 Main centres and influences involved in male sexual behaviour

The status of **pheromones** in humans is controversial. While some research has suggested that pheromonal signals underlie the observation that women living together tend to synchronise their menstrual cycles (Russell, Switz and Thompson, 1980), the research has been criticised, and others have doubted that such menstrual synchrony even occurs (Wilson, 1992). The existence in the human nose of the **vomeronasal organ** which mediates the effects of pheromones in other species has also been doubted. However, recent studies have discovered such an organ in humans which responds to direct chemical stimulation (Garcia-Velasco and Mondragon, 1991). Stern and McClintock (1998) gave women pads to wear in their armpits during different stages of the menstrual cycle. These were then given to other women to smell. The menstrual cycles of the second group of women were altered in a way that would lead to synchrony. However, there is no good evidence for pheromonal influences on sexual attraction.

Females

Sexual behaviour in female animals is affected by lesions in the anterior part of the VMH. Specifically, female rats with lesions

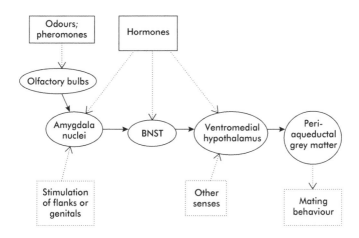

FIGURE 6.3 Main centres and influences involved in female sexual behaviour

there will not show receptive behaviour and may even attack a male rat trying to mount them. Electrical stimulation of this area produces lordosis (Pfaff and Sakuma, 1979). The sequentially dependent nature of the female response to hormones is due to their actions on cells in this area. Oestrogens cause these cells to develop progesterone receptors. Without these, the brain will not respond to progesterone, and the female rat will not adopt the receptive lordosis position. The progesterone-sensitive neurones in the VMH send fibres to the PAG in the brain stem (Hennessey *et al.*, 1990), which, as we saw in earlier chapters, is involved in the co-ordination of species-typical consummatory behaviours. Figure 6.3 gives a summary of these mechanisms.

Sexual orientation

In discussing the origins of homosexuality it is important to realise that people who engage in homosexual behaviour are not all the same. McKnight (1997) has argued that many people indulge in homosexual sex because, for example, they are experimenting, or are unable to find an opposite-sex partner. Such people are unlikely to have psychobiological characteristics in common with others who feel that they have no choice in partner selection; that same-sex partners are right for them. Failure to realise this can confuse the interpretation of research findings, and this should be kept in mind in the following discussion. The frequency of exclusive male homosexuality is less than 1 per cent in all societies studied, even though the proportion of men showing bisexuality varies enormously from one society to another (Baker and Bellis, 1995). In the following discussion we look at some possible origins of exclusive homosexuality.

Androgens

Some early studies comparing sex hormone levels in gay and straight men reported lower levels of testosterone in gays. However, later research has generally failed to confirm this (Meyer-Bahlburg, 1984) and it is thought that the earlier results might have reflected greater stress in the gay subjects. One effect of stress is to increase cortisol secretion and that in turn depresses testosterone levels. In any case, as we have seen, androgen levels are important in sexual desire and behaviour in men *and* in women, and there is no reason to suppose they should be lower in gay men.

But, even if activating effects of hormones do not differ between straight and gay people, it is possible that organising effects do. Evidence from the genetic androgen deficiencies mentioned earlier does not clearly suggest a biological rather than a socio-cultural explanation for later sexuality. In a series of papers in the 1980s, Dorner (e.g. Dorner *et al.* 1983) reported that stress in pregnancy led to increased likelihood of homosexuality in offspring, and explained this by the testosterone-reducing effect of cortisol. Previous work had shown that stress immediately before birth had these hormonal effects in rats, and also led to feminisation of the behaviour of male offspring. This type of approach to the origins of male homosexuality argues that the effect is due to *deandrogenisation* of the developing brain. We saw evidence earlier for sex differences in the CNS resulting from differences in perinatal testosterone levels. Are there differences in the brains of heterosexual and homosexual people?

Neural structures

Swaab and Hofman (1990) found that the SCN of homosexual men was about twice as large as that of heterosexual men. Since the known functions of the SCN are to do with endogenous rhythms (see Chapter 3), the significance of this is not clear. However, in subsequent studies Swaab and his colleagues have shown that the homosexual SCN differs from that of straight men specifically in having far more neurones that use vasopressin as a neurotransmitter (e.g. Zhou, Hofman and Swaab, 1995). In research with rats, they have also demonstrated that preventing perinatal testosterone acting on the brain of developing rats not only produced just this imbalance of neurone types, but also caused the rats to be bisexual in choice of sexual partner (Swaab et al., 1995).

LeVay (1991) examined post-mortem brains from gay and straight men, and from women who were assumed to be straight. He found that the INAH-3, which we saw earlier is on average twice as big in men as in women, is the same size in gay men as in women. However, there is an enormous amount of overlap in the two male distributions. Furthermore, it is possible that the difference comes about through early learning experiences, or that it is a result of, rather than a cause of, the sexual preference. What is more the result appears not to have been replicated. The sexual dimorphism of the INAH-3 is dependent on perinatal testosterone levels and so, although its role in sexual behaviour is not known, it could be the location of a deandrogenisation basis for homosexuality.

Homosexual men are also reported to have a larger anterior commissure than straight men, about the same size as that of women (Allen and Gorski, 1992). The sex difference in this structure is usually thought to relate to cognitive differences rather than differences in sexual behaviour. This is true also of differences in EEG lateralisation that have been observed between gay and straight men (Alexander and Sufka, 1993). Again, task-related EEG patterns in homosexual men are closer to those of women than to those of straight men. We will return to the significance of these cognition-related differences later.

Genetic factors

A number of studies have suggested a genetic basis for homosexuality. Studies of the families of gay people have shown that the chances of the monozygotic twin of a homosexual person being gay are at least twice as high as for a dizygotic twin. For example, Bailey and Pillard (1991) found that 50 per cent of identical twins, and 25 per cent of fraternal twins of homosexual men were also homosexual. The rates for non-twin brothers and for adoptive brothers were lower, and similar (9 per cent and 11 per cent, respectively).

Hamer *et al.* (1993) recently reported that homosexuality can be traced to a particular part of the X chromosome. While Hamer's team have replicated this result, others have failed to do so (Marshall, 1995). Hamer's methodology has been criticised; in particular, the representativeness of his sample of gay men. Not all homosexual men inherit this gene or genes, and brothers who do share the genes do not necessarily both become homosexual. It is also known that in pairs of monozygotic twins, who have exactly the same genotype, one may become gay and the other not.

Homosexuality and evolution

This discussion raises a fundamental question about a biological basis for homosexuality. It might seem that a genetic basis for homosexuality is impossible as it should directly reduce the rate of reproduction, leading to the gene dying out. In fact, there are several alternative explanations for how genes for homosexuality might be maintained in successive generations (see McKnight, 1997). One explanation is based on the concept of *balanced superior heterozygotic fitness*. According to this, an individual having one copy of a gene (being heterozygous) might gain some advantage, even if having two copies of the gene is disadvantageous. This is known to account for the occurrence in malarial areas of the genetic disease *sickle-cell anaemia*. Those who suffer from this disease have two copies of the gene responsible, but having only one copy confers some resistance to malaria on a larger number of people, and hence enhances survival of the gene in the next generation. (This example is not intended to imply that homosexuality is a disease.) One issue that such an argument leaves to be solved is: what is the advantage that this gene or these genes confer on heterozygous persons? Speculations as to what this might be mostly involve conferring some advantage in sexual performance, such as greater sexual desire, fertility or potency. Baker and Bellis (1995) suggest that heterozygocity leads to bisexuality, and provides the bisexual person with earlier and wider experience, and the opportunity to practise infidelity.

Hamer *et al.* (1993) suggested another explanation, which accounts for the gene being on the X chromosome. The action of the gene is to increase sexual desire for male partners. In women this has direct consequences for reproductive performance and leads to greater representation of the gene in the next generation. The effect in men, to increase the likelihood of homosexual behaviour, is simply a spin-off. Whatever the true picture, the assumption that homosexuality is counter to evolutionary success is clearly based on a simplistic view of genetics and evolution.

On the other hand, it is also simplistic to imagine that the genetic basis of homosexuality depends on a single gene. Bem (1996) has proposed that what brain structures, hormones and genes actually determine is childhood *temperament*, and this in turn leads to the development of attraction to those who seem different from oneself, either same- or other-sex individuals. This is consistent with the findings reported earlier of homosexual–heterosexual differences in structures that are related to cognitive functioning, rather than directly to sexual behaviour. This theory suggests that same- and opposite-sex preferences are determined in exactly the same way, and attempts to integrate physiological and socio-cultural factors in the development of sexuality.

Summary

Human beings are sexually dimorphic: that is, men and women have bodies that are structurally different. This sexual dimorphism results from the organising effects of testosterone on the male embryo, and at puberty from androgens in males and oestrogens in females. Sexual behaviour of most species depends on 'sex-appropriate' hormones. Gonadectomy of male and female animals results in complete loss of sexual interest and behaviour. These are reinstated by appropriate replacement of hormones. Testosterone acts with a permissive effect on pre-programmed sexual behaviour of males. Testosterone has a similar role in men, but some men continue to be sexually active after castration. Women's sexual desire and behaviour are independent of female sex hormones but are probably related to testosterone. The organising effects of testosterone produce structural differences in the brains of males and females, and permit the body to react to later activating effects. Male homosexuality has been attributed by some to insufficient androgenisation of the developing brain, possibly as a result of maternal stress. The brains of homosexual men are more like those of women than those of other men, although the differences seem to relate to cognitive processes rather than directly to sexual behaviour. A genetic influence on homosexuality has also been proposed.

Further reading

Baker, R. R. and Bellis, M. A. (1995) *Human Sperm Competition: Copulation, Masturbation and Infidelity*, London: Chapman and Hall. Baker and Bellis apply the sociobiological approach to human sexual behaviour in a provocative but scholarly work.

Brannon, L. (1996) *Gender, Psychological Perspectives*, Boston/London: Allyn and Bacon. A wide-ranging account of gender differences (from emotions to aptitude for work) and theories proposed to explain them (from psychoanalysis to hormones and brain structures).

McKnight, J. (1997) *Straight Science? Homosexuality, Evolution and Adaptation*, London: Routledge. Jim McKnight provides a thorough account of alternative explanations for the evolutionary potential of homosexuality, and an excellent overview of its hormonal, neural and familial aspects. At the same time, he cautions strongly against the over-zealous application of socio-biological arguments to human social behaviour.

Chapter 7

Aggression

Biology of aggression

Aggressive behaviour is widespread in the animal kingdom. Like all other biologically based behaviour, it ultimately serves to increase the proportion of the organism's genes which are passed on to the next generation. This underlying principle is not quite so clear in the case of aggression as we have seen it to be for sex, but aggression can usually be interpreted as serving the aims of reproduction. As with sex we will see that aggressive behaviour is *species-typical*, is controlled by *neural circuits*, is heavily influenced by *organising and activating effects of sex hormones* and, in human beings, is largely freed of these biological constraints. It may also be *sexually dimorphic*.

Types of aggression

Aggressive behaviours have been classified in different ways. One useful, functional classification has distinguished three types of aggressive behaviour. First is **offensive aggression,** which is aggressive behaviour involving attacks of one animal on another. Second is **defensive aggression,** aggressive behaviour when attacked or threatened. Third is **predation,** aggressive behaviour directed at a member of another species, usually for food. In most species studied, offensive and defensive aggression have many features in common, although they are not identical. Cats, for example, employ back-arching, hair-raising and hissing in both offensive and defensive displays, the main difference appearing to be postural. In rats, the behaviours are more different and easily distinguished on the basis of specific components of the behaviour. Both offensive and defensive behaviour are accompanied by high levels of sympathetic activation.

Offensive and defensive behaviour usually involve multiple or prolonged threat displays and more than one attack. The end result is usually the withdrawal of one or other of the combatants, often before the confrontation has escalated from threat to actual attack. Predatory behaviour is very different. In this, the animal seems to make itself as unobtrusive as possible (e.g. the cat stalking with its belly close to the ground). The actual attack behaviour is directed at killing the victim and usually consists of a single attack without threat displays. Predation usually ends with a single fatal bite or with the predator giving up. Since predation is so different some have considered it to be more appropriately viewed as feeding rather than aggressive behaviour. We shall be concentrating in this chapter on offensive and defensive aggression.

Sexual dimorphism of aggression

The patterns of aggressive behaviour in male and female animals seem to be the same, and we will assume that the neural circuits underlying them are the same. However, the nature of aggression does differ between the sexes. Most aggression is directly related to reproduction. As male and female animals have different reproductive roles, aggression serves different immediate ends for male and female animals. These sex-specific roles vary from species to species. In some, males maintain territories (and their resident female or females) which they protect by aggressive displays towards other males. In other species males have to compete for mating rights with the females, even if this does not involve territory. This competition involves inter-male aggression. It is no accident that the mating displays in many species, directed towards a female, are very similar to aggressive displays directed towards competitor males. Females in a few species also have to compete with other females, for example for nesting sites. More usually, however, female aggression is defensive and is deployed in the defence of the young.

Neural mechanisms

The three types of aggressive behaviour seem to have different central mechanisms. As with the other types of motivated behaviour we have looked at, such as feeding and sex, the specific behaviours involved are controlled by centres in the midbrain. These specific motor circuits are controlled by centres in the hypothalamus and in the limbic system, especially in the amygdala. Although stimulation studies as far back as the 1920s showed that these areas are involved, it is only in the past 20 years that a clear picture of the separate control of different types of aggression has started to emerge, although a lot of detail is still not known. The differences between offensive and defensive (and predatory) behaviour have allowed researchers to separate the neural mechanisms involved using lesion and stimulation methods.

Offensive aggression

The species-typical motor pattern of offensive aggression is programmed by neurones in the **ventral tegmental area** of the midbrain (see Figure 7.1). Lesions in this region prevent the occurrence of offensive aggression, but not defensive aggression or predation (Adams, 1986). Stimulation of this area produces species-typical offensive aggressive behaviour. These neurones receive inputs from the *anterior hypothalamus*. Stimulation of parts of the anterior hypothalamus leads to offensive attack. However, *lesions* of the anterior hypothalamus *do not* abolish offensive behaviour, but may change its probability of occurring in the presence of particular sorts of stimuli, such as a male of the same species (e.g. Ellison and Flynn, 1968). So, it seems that the anterior hypothalamus normally plays a role in determining the occurrence of aggressive behaviour, but it does not directly initiate the behaviour. Most of the research underlying these results shows that attack depends on the animal receiving certain types of stimulation, most obviously the presence of another animal or sometimes tactile stimulation of limbs or face.

Cortical centres exert inhibitory control over offensive aggression. Removal of the cerebral cortex of cats results in uncontrolled 'sham rage', which appears to be offensive aggression, and alcohol reduces the inhibition. Inhibitory influences on offensive aggression have been shown to be mediated by 5-HT neurones

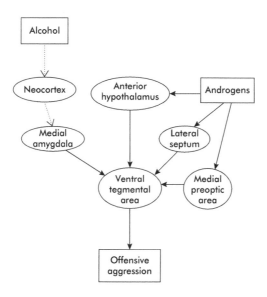

FIGURE 7.1 Some possible mechanisms involved in offensive aggression

in, amongst other places, the *MPA* (Cologer-Clifford *et al.*, 1997). A number of studies have linked violent crime in humans with lesions in the temporal lobe, including people with temporal lobe epilepsy (see Mark and Ervin, 1970).

Defensive aggression

The motor programmes for defensive aggression are located in neurones in the *periaqueductal grey matter* (PAG) of the midbrain (see Figure 7.2). Defensive behaviour consisting of threat displays seems to be controlled separately from that involving actual attack behaviour (Carrive, Bandler and Dampney, 1989). The hypothalamic and limbic circuits that control the PAG programmes have been summarised by Siegel, Schubert and Shaikh (1997). Their direct activation is by amino acid-based neurones from the *medial hypothalamus*, which themselves are excited by inputs from the *medial amygdala*. This activation is modulated by direct inputs to the PAG from the amygdala: an opioid, inhibitory one

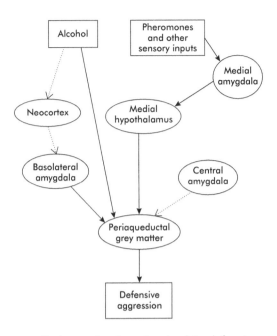

FIGURE 7.2 Brain mechanisms involved in defensive aggression

from the *central amygdala*; and an amino acid, excitatory one from the *basal complex*. Alcohol has stimulating effects on aggression not only by reducing the inhibitory influence of the cerebral cortex, but also by directly stimulating the pathway between the medial hypothalamus and the PAG. The amygdala itself receives multiple inputs, notably direct afferent inputs from the olfactory system and from other sensory systems. It also contains neurones which possess receptors for oestrogens and androgens.

Hormones in aggression

Non-human studies

We saw in Chapter 6 how perinatal testosterone levels have an organising effect on adult sexual behaviour, in particular on the sexual response to adult hormone levels. Research on the organising effects of perinatal hormones on *offensive* aggression shows that they parallel the sexual effects almost exactly. In normal rats, for example, males show far more offensive behaviour than do females. Male aggression is almost entirely directed at other males. Such inter-male aggression in rodents starts at the time of puberty, just when androgen secretion starts to rise, and pre-pubertal mice can be made aggressive by injections of testosterone (McKinney and Desjardins, 1973). Rats castrated at birth do not respond to testosterone with increased aggression, while those castrated in adult life respond rapidly.

Aggressive behaviour in male rats is also affected by social or situational factors, and this, too, interacts with sex hormones. A male rat housed with a female shows more aggressive behaviour when tested by confrontation with a strange male rat than does a rat housed alone or with another male. This effect is increased if the animals are treated with testosterone (Albert *et al.*, 1988). Thus, the presence of the female sensitises the male rat to the effects of testosterone. Similarly, castrated rats who were made to compete for a food source not only competed more strongly if they were administered testosterone, but also subsequently attacked a docile, strange rat *only* if they had both testosterone and this previous competitive experience. Thus, the offensive aggression depended on both experience *and* testosterone (Albert, Petrovic and Walsh, 1989).

While offensive aggression is rare in female rodents it does occur and occurs to different degrees in different individuals. This is, again, related to activating and organising effects of androgens. An activating effect is shown, for example, when adult females respond to testosterone injections with increased inter-female aggression (van de Poll *et al.*, 1988). The organising effect is shown in the individual differences in natural response, and in response to adult testosterone injections. These result from differing degrees of exposure to androgens as foetuses. Because rats have large litters a female foetus will be alongside different numbers of male foetuses (from none to two). It has been shown that those alongside two males have higher testosterone levels, and that they respond more to adult testosterone injection than those alongside none (vom Saal,

1983). Their exposure to higher levels of androgens *in utero* has a masculinising effect.

The main occurrence of female offensive aggression in most species is what is called *maternal aggression*. In species where the female is devoted to care of the young, attack on a stranger is immediate and fierce. In rodents, this increased aggressiveness builds up during pregnancy and parallels the gradual increase in levels of progesterone (Mann, Konen and Svare, 1984). Although the progesterone level drops late in pregnancy the aggressiveness continues. It has been postulated that this is the result of an increase in testosterone just before the female gives birth. This aggression is, however, suspended for a short period immediately after they have given birth (which allows them to mate again without attacking the male), and this seems to result from a suppressing effect of oestradiol, which is secreted at that time (Svare, 1989). The aggressive response also depends on the presence of the young; if they are removed, the female will not attack intruders.

Female aggression in some species has been shown to relate to hormonal changes in the oestrus cycle. Thus, female hamsters are aggressive except when in the receptive phase of their oestrus cycle. Ovariectomy renders them continuously aggressive. Injection of both oestrogen and progesterone not only reinstates their sexual behaviour but eliminates their aggressiveness (Floody and Pfaff, 1977). This clear relation with female hormones is unusual, however.

Wallen (1996) has argued, on the basis of a review of studies of early social and hormonal effects on rhesus monkeys, that environmental factors are the main influence on aggressive behaviour in primates. Specifically, whether monkeys are submissive, or dominant and aggressive depends more on the level of aggression in the environment in which they are reared than on the individual's level of circulating androgens. Some primates show variations in aggressiveness during the menstrual cycle, and the part of the cycle varies too. In some it is greatest at the time of ovulation, in others immediately before menstruation.

The activating effects of androgens on aggression are mediated through receptors in several of the brain areas we looked at in the previous section, notably in the amygdala, the medial hypo-thalamus, the MPA and the lateral septum. There is also evidence of oestrogen receptors in the MPA which reduce aggressive behav-iour (Cologer-Clifford *et al.*, 1997).

Human aggression

Can we draw any parallels from this brief survey of animal research for human aggression? Certain parallels are obvious, but at the same time the differences are enormous. Aggression is far more frequent in men than in women. Hyde (1986), in a review of a large number of studies, showed that this difference was large in pre-school-age children, moderate in 9–12-year-olds and small in young adults. Eagly and Steffen (1986) in a similar review revealed that the sex difference was largest for physical violence and small-est when subjects believed that their behaviour was unobserved, suggesting a strong social influence on the sex difference.

However, we should not rule out the effects of perinatal testosterone influencing the sex difference, since its organising effects are, as we saw in Chapter 6, clear in sexual behaviour. But evidence to assess this is hard to come by in humans. Reinisch (1981) showed that boys and girls whose mothers had been administered a synthetic androgen drug in pregnancy to prevent miscarriage were more aggressive than others whose mothers were not so treated. On the other hand, studies of girls with adreno-genital syndrome (see Chapter 6) have not shown a clear effect on aggression, although in other respects the girls behaved like boys (they were described as 'tomboys'; Ehrhardt and Meyer-Bahlburg, 1981).

Human male aggression, like that of other species, increases at puberty along with increased testosterone secretion. Much of the research on humans suffers from methodological problems and ethical constraints. It is known that castration of adult men not only decreases sexual urges, as I mentioned in Chapter 6, but also decreases aggressiveness. Van Goozen *et al.* (1995) showed that female-to-male transsexuals, being treated with androgens, gave greater aggressive responses to imagined frustration than controls, while male-to-female transsexuals, being treated with androgen blockers, became less aggressive.

Correlational studies to see if individual differences in aggressiveness relate to individual differences in androgens generally, but not always, show some such correlation. A number of studies have shown that people convicted of violent crimes have higher testosterone levels than those convicted of non-violent crimes. This is true of men (e.g. Dabbs *et al.*, 1987) and of women (e.g. Dabbs and Hargrove, 1997). In most studies these relationships are small, and we have to remember two main difficulties of interpreting correlational studies. First, they do not directly address the direction of cause and effect (increased androgen levels might *result from* aggression, in the way that increased androgen levels can *result from* sexual activity, see Chapter 6). Second, they do not rule out other, co-varying factors which might give the appearance of a direct relationship.

Thus, for example, an increasing number of studies suggest that the relation is actually between *dominance* and testosterone, rather than aggression and testosterone, and further, that the testosterone difference may be a *result* of changes in dominance, not a cause. For example, Ehrenkranz, Bliss and Sheard (1974) compared three groups: chronically aggressive convicts of violent crimes; dominant but non-aggressive convicts of non-violent crimes; and non-aggressive, non-dominant controls. The first two groups were found to have equally high levels of testosterone, both higher than the third group. A series of studies by Mazur and Lamb (1980) confirmed this. In one, testosterone levels were higher in men who had won a tennis match easily than in those who had won narrowly. Further, testosterone levels were elevated in those winning prizes as a result of their own efforts (students graduating), but not in those who won as no result of their own ability (lottery winners). Schaal *et al.* (1996) followed a group of boys from the age of six to thirteen, assessing aggressiveness throughout and dominance and testosterone levels at the end. Boys perceived as dominant had higher testosterone levels, but those with a history of physical aggression actually had *lower* testosterone levels. This same interpretation could apply to correlational studies in animals. Animals higher in a **dominance hierarchy** show higher levels of testosterone. However, this may be due to the fact that they fight more, to the fact that they win more fights or simply to their dominant position.

There is less evidence of relationships between female hormones and aggression although, as we saw earlier, one or two pieces of evidence suggest that higher levels of oestrogen suppress aggression in females of certain species. The evidence relating to increased aggressiveness immediately before menstruation in women, as part of what has been labelled a pre-menstrual syndrome (PMS), is far from conclusive. Van Goozen *et al.* (1996) have shown that anger is more easily aroused in the pre-menstrual phase, but only for those women who previously complained of irritability in the pre-menstrual phase. A significantly higher level of cortisol in these women on the day of testing led to the tentative conclusion that those women showing greater irritability are more stress-prone.

So, the conclusion about aggression has to be similar to that about sexual behaviour. While human aggressive behaviour shows some of the relationships to hormonal function shown in the animals most closely studied, i.e. rodents and cats, the relationship is much looser. Further, human aggression seems to be much less species-typical than that of the other species. That is, once again the type of behaviour is subject to greater individual control than is that of the other species.

Sex and aggression

From the preceding sections, it should be apparent that offensive aggression is linked to sexual and reproductive activities. Zillmann (1989) has explored further the connections between sex and aggression and has extended these more directly into human behaviour. His interest in this stems from research on the effects of pornography, in which he noted that sexual and violent stimuli frequently have similar effects on viewers. His basic assumption is that sex and aggression are both associated with sympathetic arousal, and that both increase in intensity with greater arousal.

Arousal may transfer from one to the other. Thus, unexpressed annoyance fosters later sexual response, and unexpressed sexual arousal can enhance subsequent sexual arousal and/or aggression (see Zillmann, 1989). Other common features involve cognitive processes. Cognitive control may be exerted over both aggression and sexual behaviour, while, conversely, both aggression and sexual arousal may, if sufficiently intense, interfere with cognitive processes, particularly in narrowing attention to the object of the aggression or sexual behaviour.

In humans, the relation between aggression and sex goes beyond the biological role of the one achieving the other, although it may be seen to have its origin in this role. Thus, aggression is not uncommonly used by men in most cultures to force unwilling females into having sex (i.e. rape). As has already been pointed out, many of the effects of viewing pornography are indistinguishable from the effects of viewing violence, possibly because of the common involvement of sympathetic arousal. Sadomasochistic sexual interactions depend on aggressive acts enhancing sexual experience. More commonly, sexual activity is accompanied by actions with an aggressive origin, such as biting and scratching.

Temporal lobe disorders also seem to link sex and aggression. We saw in Chapter 6 how temporal lobe lesions in humans and animals are associated with unusual sexual behaviour. Earlier in this chapter, we mentioned the reported association between temporal lobe disorders and violent behaviour (see p. 111). There is some evidence that the two frequently co-occur. Langevin and his colleagues (1985) have shown that more than the expected number of sadists have temporal lobe disorders.

Summary

Offensive and defensive aggression clearly serve reproductive functions in the animal world. While male and female animals show similar motor patterns in aggressive behaviour, these serve different functions related to the reproductive functions of the sexes of a particular species. Offensive and defensive aggression are subserved by different, but closely related, neural circuits in the limbic system, hypothalamus and brain stem. The sexual dimorphism of aggression in rodents is largely the result of organising effects of perinatal androgens. In both sexes androgens also have activating effects on offensive aggression. Maternal aggression in rodents is dependent on female sex hormones as well as on testosterone. Endocrine effects on primate, including human, aggression are much less marked than in rodents. Social factors have a profound effect on the expression of aggression in humans. Men are more aggressive than women in most situations, but the sex difference is larger in young children and smallest in women who believe that they are unobserved. Weak correlations are found between levels of testosterone and aggression in male and female criminals. However, the relation is more likely to be with dominance, often served by aggression, than by aggression itself. Relations between sexual behaviour and aggression are clear in humans, and may be based on common features like arousal and proximity of neural systems.

Further reading

Archer, J. and Browne, K. (1989) *Human Aggression: Naturalistic Approaches*, London: Routledge. As its title suggests, this volume concentrates on non-laboratory studies of the effect of social context on aggression in humans.

Englander, E. K. (1997) *Understanding Violence*, Mahwah, NJ: Lawrence Erlbaum. This book gives a wide-ranging survey of research on human aggression of different types and attempts a synthesis of genetic and environmental factors.

Chapter 8

Reward and addiction

General principles of drug action

A drug is a substance which directly alters the function of the body. Most of the drugs that we use are therapeutic drugs; we take them, for example, to kill micro-organisms or to correct biochemical imbalances in our tissues. Some drugs are **psychoactive**; that is, they change the individual's psychological state. This term could include classes of drugs such as pain-killers but is most often restricted to drugs which change mood or which produce hallucinations.

Most of us use psychoactive drugs. *Caffeine* and related stimulant drugs are present in coffee, tea, cola drinks and chocolate. *Alcohol*, a CNS depressant, and *nicotine*, a stimulant, are very widely used drugs. The language used to describe psychoactive drugs and their use is rarely neutral. Describing them as *recreational drugs* gives them a positive connotation, while referring to *drugs of abuse* clearly has negative meaning. This negative meaning can derive from moral, social or legal considerations, or combinations of these. The legal status of drugs does far more than invite the use of different language. It also has an enormous practical significance on the consequences of drug use. The legally available drugs alcohol and nicotine are undeniably more dangerous than drugs like *marijuana* and *ecstasy*, not only because of their wider use, but also because of their extremely serious injurious effects. Many of the dangers of the use of illegal drugs derive from the criminalisation of those who use and provide them, and were seen in the case of alcohol during the prohibition era in the USA.

Psychoactive drugs are sometimes described as being either *soft* or *hard* drugs. Although this distinction carries many connotations, at core it relates to the ease with which a drug causes **addiction**. Addiction is a powerful, and often destructive, form of motivation, which is generally viewed as having a physiological basis. In order to understand addiction we need to look first at the general properties of drugs.

Tolerance

Prolonged or repeated administration of most drugs leads to **drug tolerance**. Tolerance is a state of decreased sensitivity to the effects of a drug. As a consequence of this decreased sensitivity the dose needs to be increased to overcome the effect of tolerance in order to get the required effect of the drug. Most drugs have more than one action (e.g. *cocaine* is a local anaesthetic, it speeds up the heart and some motor responses, and it leads to pleasant feelings). If the effects are unwanted, we call them side-effects. Tolerance does not develop at the same rate to different effects of drugs, and may not develop at all to some effects. This is of enormous importance in relation to the use of particular psychoactive drugs. For example, tolerance to the euphoric effect of opiates like *heroin* usually develops more rapidly than tolerance to the physical effects. Tolerance to the nauseating effects of alcohol or tobacco develops rapidly, but tolerance to other effects (such as inebriation) develops more slowly. Tolerance to the hypnotic (sleep-inducing) and sedative (relaxing) effects of *barbiturates* is not accompanied by any change in the fatal dose. The result in each case is that users have to increase the dose of the drug to get the same desired psychological effect but, in doing so, subject themselves to greater unwanted side-effects, some of which may be dangerous or fatal.

Drug tolerance is of two broad types. **Metabolic tolerance** is a reduction in the amount of the drug reaching its sites of action. Usually, this is the result of increased metabolism of the drug in places such as the liver. **Functional tolerance** is a reduction in reactivity of the sites of action, caused by changes in the structure or number of receptor sites, or changes in the structure of cell membranes. Tolerance to psychoactive drugs is mostly functional.

While functional tolerance is mainly a result of biochemical or biomechanical changes it is also affected by learning processes.

In particular, it has been shown that tolerance to particular drug effects depends on *experiencing the effect*, rather than simply on receiving the drug. This is known as **contingent drug tolerance**. For example, alcohol has an anticonvulsive effect, reducing convulsions that result from electric shocks to the head. In a study by Pinel, Mana and Kim (1989), one group of rats received alcohol before each of a series of shocks. This initially stopped the convulsions, but over a number of trials, as drug tolerance built up, led to the animals experiencing convulsions of increasing duration. In contrast, a second group received the same number of alcohol injections, but received them *after* the shocks, so that they did not experience any anticonvulsive effect. When tested by the administration of alcohol *before* the shock in a final trial this second group of rats had convulsions completely blocked, in contrast to the first group who showed almost no anticonvulsive action of alcohol. So, despite the fact that the rats in both groups were given the same number of shocks and the same number of alcohol injections, tolerance only developed in those animals in whom the alcohol was allowed to have an anticonvulsive effect; that is, those who experienced the effect of the drug.

Perhaps more important is **situational specificity of drug tolerance**. In one study (Crowell, Hinson and Siegel, 1981), tolerance to another effect of alcohol was examined, that is its property of reducing body temperature. A group of rats received alternating daily injections of alcohol and saline, but received them in two different, distinctive cages. After twenty injections all animals showed complete tolerance of the alcohol effect; that is, there was no lowering of body temperature when alcohol was injected. However, this only occurred when they were tested in the place they had previously always received alcohol injections. When they were re-tested with alcohol injections in the room in which they had previously received only saline, there was a complete absence of tolerance; temperature dropped just as much as it had on the first day. Thus, tolerance was specific to the situation in which it had developed.

The importance of this is that human recreational drug users develop tolerance to their drug, and so have to increase the dose to get the same effect. If this tolerance develops in a particular place, then injecting the higher level of the drug in a novel location is accompanied by a higher risk of death from overdose; that is, overdose is situation-specific. This, too, has been demonstrated directly with rats. Rats that had developed tolerance to heroin injections were administered a higher dose. Those that received it in a novel environment were 50 per cent more likely to die than those who received it in the usual place (Siegel *et al.*, 1982). Drug tolerance leads directly to **withdrawal symptoms.** These are in general the opposite effects to those that the drug produces. For example, heroin produces euphoria and relaxation, and its withdrawal results in depression and anxiety, while the withdrawal of sleeping pills leads to insomnia. It is assumed that withdrawal symptoms result from compensatory changes built up during tolerance. Siegel (1978) has described how these compensatory changes become conditioned to environmental cues associated with drug taking, including people, places and equipment. The presence of these cues will increase the intensity of the withdrawal symptoms.

Dependence and addiction

Drug dependence is a state in which an individual requires a drug in order to function normally. For example, epileptics are dependent on the anticonvulsant drugs they take; if they stop taking them, they suffer convulsions. Similarly, people who suffer from insulin-dependent diabetes will pass into a coma and die if they do not receive insulin injections. The similarity between withdrawal of a drug on which a person is dependent, and one to which tolerance has built up following recreational use has suggested that dependence is the basis of addiction. The term 'dependence' has frequently been used as if it were synonymous with 'addiction'. However, while addiction and dependence do often go together there are good reasons for treating the two as separate processes. It is possible to be dependent on a substance without being addicted to it. It is not useful, for example, to consider that the epileptic and the diabetic are addicted to anticonvulsants and insulin.

So, what is addiction? It is important to distinguish between addiction and dependence because such a distinction actually helps us to understand the causes of addiction. For the purposes of this chapter I shall adopt the following definition: *addiction is a state characterised by an overwhelming involvement with the use of a drug, and a high tendency to relapse into using the drug after stopping.*

Mechanisms of addiction

Physical dependence theory

The most widely accepted explanation for addiction was, for a long time, the physical dependence theory. The argument is that once a drug has been taken long enough to induce tolerance (equated with dependence), stopping taking the drug leads to withdrawal symptoms. Since withdrawal symptoms are aversive, addicts maintain their addiction to avoid withdrawal symptoms. Treatments for addiction that stem from this position are based on gradual reduction of drug doses. In alcoholism treatment, in particular, this process is known as **detoxification**. If addiction is maintained by the avoidance of withdrawal symptoms, then getting a person past the stage of symptoms should be effective in the long term, preventing relapse. Unfortunately the results are not good: a high proportion of addicts start taking the drug again (Pickens and Fletcher, 1991).

There are other reasons for rejecting the physical dependence view of addiction. Addicts do not necessarily maintain a constant blood level of the drug, as a withdrawal-based theory would predict. Frequently, they involve themselves in cycles of bingeing and withdrawal (whether voluntarily, to fit in with a 'normal' social and working life, or by necessity from poverty or incarceration). This 'naturally occurring' sort of detoxification does not result in loss of the addiction. It is now clear that addiction does not necessarily involve dependence. There is no clear relation between a drug's potential for dependence and tolerance on the one hand, and the likelihood of it causing addiction on the other. Cocaine, for example, is highly addictive, but does not produce much tolerance, nor very serious withdrawal symptoms. Conversely, dependence does not necessarily lead to addiction, as is shown clearly with many therapeutic drugs. The dependence model does not give an account of why addiction starts in the first place. The final reason comes from studies of localised drug actions in animals.

Earlier, I pointed out that any one drug has more than one effect. This is because a drug attaches to receptors in different locations, producing effects that depend on the location. Although the euphoric effects of opiates are by way of their action in the **mesolimbic dopamine system** (**MDS**, which we will look at later), their other actions result from attaching to receptors elsewhere. For example, the analgesic effect results from attachment to receptors in the PAG. Rats can be trained to self-administer opiates into the MDS and effectively may be considered addicted. Stopping the self-administration does not result in withdrawal symptoms. However, if opiates are repeatedly injected into the PAG, then withdrawal symptoms *do* follow the cessation of injections (Bozarth and Wise, 1984). This shows that the mechanisms for the positive reinforcing (and presumably addictive) consequences of opiate injection and those of the negative consequences of withdrawal are separate.

However, we must not discard the notion of avoidance of withdrawal entirely, since it is certainly the case that addicts in the throes of withdrawal are usually desperate to obtain their drug to put an end to their symptoms.

Positive incentive theory

More recently, a positive incentive theory has gradually gained wide acceptance. This approach claims that addiction is maintained not by the avoidance of unpleasant consequences of withdrawal, but rather by the *rewarding* consequences of taking the drug. That is, people become addicted to the positive effects of the drug, rather than to avoidance of the negative consequences of withdrawal. But lots of behaviours are rewarding, and while some of these have been described as addictive (and we will examine these on pp. 133–4), most theories agree that drug addiction is somehow different. The physiological basis of addiction, according to positive incentive theory, lies in dopaminergic circuits in the midbrain and forebrain.

Central reward circuits

Intracranial self-stimulation

Olds and Milner (1954) implanted electrodes into midbrain regions of rats, and arranged that every time a rat pressed a lever in the experimental cage it caused a brief burst of electrical current to pass to the tip of the electrode. The rats rapidly learned to press the lever and responded very quickly. So, the electrical stimulation had the properties of a reward, reinforcing the immediately preceding behaviour, bar pressing. Later work has shown similar results in other species, including humans. In people, self-stimulation is experienced usually as non-specifically pleasurable, although it is sometimes reported to be sexual in nature. The most important network involved in the supposed central reward circuits is the mesolimbic dopamine system. The *medial forebrain bundle*, which is where Olds and Milner placed their electrodes, seems now most likely to be simply a pathway transferring information from one part of the system (the substantia nigra and the ventral tegmental area) to others (the **nucleus accumbens**, the amygdala and the prefrontal cortex amongst others).

Olds and Milner claimed that the locations they found are the natural reward circuits of the brain. That is, what they were doing in the self-stimulation studies was to 'short-circuit' the usual learning process by omitting an external source of reward. The acceptance of this view has waxed and waned over the years as it was first noted that this learning seemed to have different properties to learning rewarded by external sources. Subsequently, it was demonstrated that the apparent differences are artifacts of the different experimental set-ups. In particular, the animals in self-stimulation studies were not in states of deprivation, they lacked appropriate goal objects and had no delay between response and reward. When these differences are removed, externally rewarded behaviour is much more like self-stimulation (e.g. Panksepp and Trowill, 1967). Similarities also appear between the consequences of external rewards, and chemical stimulation and blocking of parts of the MDS. The view that the stimulated areas are the usual reward circuits subsequently became dominant again. However, Salamone, Cousins and Snyder (1997) have recently summarised evidence that suggests that the MDS circuits involved are not those responsible for natural reinforcement. They argue that the parallels between the effects of stimulation and receptor-blocking drugs on these circuits and the effects of external reward and extinction are superficial, and on closer examination are different. Furthermore, these networks are also involved in aversive responses so do not solely serve a positive reward mechanism. However, they do agree that these networks are the basis of addiction and other rewarding effects of drugs.

The neural basis of addiction

It is argued that what the addictive drugs have in common, and this is not shared with non-addictive drugs, is that they act on these dopaminergic circuits (see Koob and Bloom, 1988). There is plenty of direct evidence for this. For example, laboratory animals will learn to inject minute quantities of opiates into parts of the reward system (e.g. Bozarth and Wise, 1984). Injection of opiate antagonists directly into the nucleus accumbens and the ventral tegmental area results in increased intravenous self-administration (e.g. Vaccarino, Bloom and Koob, 1985). Many other results of the rewarding properties of opiates, and of addictive stimulants like amphetamines, are disrupted by local manipulations of the dopamine reward systems.

Opiates, cocaine, amphetamines, alcohol and nicotine all act on neurones in the dopaminergic reward system, and this is the basis of the positive incentive theory of addiction (Wise and

Bozarth, 1987). They do this in various ways, for example by stimulating the dopamine receptors (opiates), or increasing the release of dopamine into synapses (cocaine and alcohol). The fact that these substances all act on the same central system suggests that we should look for interactions between them. In laboratory studies rats have been trained to self-administer opiates or cocaine, the reinforcing drug is then removed, resulting in the eventual extinction of the behaviour. It has been found that injecting other dopamine agonists causes the behaviour to recommence. This might well be the explanation for the fact that tobacco smoking or alcohol drinking can promote relapse in addicts who have stopped taking their drug (Stewart and Brown, 1995).

White (1996) has summarised recent research and arguments against the MDS being the sole location for the CNS changes in addiction. In his view, natural reinforcers operate in multiple memory systems in the brain, especially in the amygdala and hippocampus, and the evidence demonstrates that different classes of addictive substances modulate the activity of these systems in different ways.

Individual differences

The positive incentive theory has limitations. First, it is clear that avoidance of withdrawal symptoms plays an important role, and proponents of the positive incentive approach accept this. Second, it does not account for individual differences in drug response. Why do most people who try drugs not go on to become addicted, and may even be able to use drugs for an extended period without doing so, while others are hooked almost immediately? Similarly, only a minority of patients given regular treatment with opiates to relieve pain during hospital treatment become addicted. There is no simple explanation for this, but in this section we will look at some contributory factors.

Genetic factors

Several studies have implicated genetic factors in predisposing people to addiction. The monozygotic (identical) twin of an alcoholic is twice as likely to be alcoholic as a dizygotic (fraternal) twin (e.g. Goodwin, 1979). While this could, at least in part, be explained by the tendency for monozygotic twins to be treated more similarly than dizygotic ones, the role of inheritance is further shown by adoption studies. Children of alcoholics adopted in infancy by non-alcoholic parents are more likely to become alcoholics themselves than are children of non-alcoholics similarly adopted (Goodwin *et al.*, 1973). Cloninger (1987) has argued that inheritance has its clearest effect in the case of drinking which involves prolonged, steady consumption of alcohol. Other drinkers with an alcohol problem could be described as binge drinkers. They indulge in occasional bouts of very high levels of alcohol intake, but between bouts can abstain for long periods. The evidence suggests that the children of binge drinkers only themselves become binge drinkers if they are exposed to a binge-drinking environment. Since, according to our working definition of addiction, binge drinkers would probably not be described as addicted, this does not detract from the evidence of the importance of genetic factors in addiction.

Personality

Other individual predisposing factors may be viewed as personality traits. Some psychodynamic theorists have argued that there is an *addictive personality* which makes people especially vulnerable to addiction. This is chiefly characterised by dependence, initially on other people, but eventually on drugs. Other features are that addiction-prone people are described as impulsive, anti-social and novelty-seeking.

Although these issues have mostly been investigated by psychoanalytic and self-report questionnaire techniques, possible physiological substrates have been suggested. Cloninger (1987) has pointed out that many studies of people with impulsive, antisocial traits, who are susceptible to alcohol addiction, have shown that they have low levels of the breakdown products of 5-HT and dopamine in their cerebrospinal fluids. He suggested that the dopamine deficit shows these people have underactive reward systems causing them to seek sensation, including that afforded by drugs. Simultaneously, the 5-HT deficit suggests underactivity in the serotonergic systems that modulate the effects of aversive stimuli, making them less responsive to punishment and social disapproval. A related construct, more widely discussed in social psychology, is that of *self-esteem*, and people who become addicted have been described as having previously suffered from low self-esteem. Huebner (1993) has suggested that low self-esteem can be related to underactivity of reward mechanisms, and that eating disorders, which are characterised by low self-esteem, can be viewed as a form of addictive behaviour.

Socio-cultural factors

Drug use and consequential addiction are more common when families or social groups tolerate drug use, and especially when it is an important of family or social culture (Walsh, 1992). Alcohol and nicotine addiction are far more widespread than opiate addiction because our society tolerates (we could even say *encourages* through widespread advertising) the use of these substances. Drug use is also more prevalent when individuals are subject to stress from family or social sources, so that it is common in areas of social deprivation, and in groups with lower socio-economic status (Smith, North and Spitznagel, 1993).

Interpersonal factors in the family, such as modelling of drug use by parents, or less specifically the provision of a stressful family environment, also predispose the individual to the use of drugs. Some have attempted to explain drug use and addiction entirely by reference to such socio-cultural factors (e.g. Walsh, 1992). However, this is to ignore the relevance of all the other factors we have looked at in this chapter, and we should conclude that socio-cultural factors interact with other personal and biological factors in the production of addiction.

Non-chemical addiction

The final point to consider is whether the concept of addiction can be applied to things other than the ingestion of drugs. Many authorities have applied the term to a wide range of behaviours, including gambling, sex, shopping, exercise, computer games and recently surfing the Internet. In everyday language the term is used even more widely. The definition of addiction that I quoted earlier limits the use of the term to the taking of drugs. However, if we leave the reference to a drug out of the definition I gave earlier, then it makes perfect sense to apply it to behaviours such as those I have listed above. For example, Rosenthal and Lesieur (1992) showed that pathological gamblers show behaviour similar to tolerance (increasing time spent gambling and increasing size of stake), report withdrawal symptoms (craving, insomnia, headaches and palpitations) and have a high tendency to relapse.

But is this more than an analogy? It only makes sense to talk of gambling and heroin addiction as the same type of behaviour if we can show that they share more than superficial similarities, although the deeper connections may be physiological or psychological. Just as drug addicts frequently use more than one drug, so gambling and drug use tend to go together. Linden, Pope and Jonas (1986) showed that half of their sample of Gamblers Anonymous attenders reported problems with alcohol or other drugs, while Lesieur, Bloom and Zoppa (1986) showed that 20 per cent of a large sample of alcoholics and other drug addicts also had problems with gambling. Bergh *et al.* (1997) examined neurotransmitter action in pathological gamblers. They found an increased release of dopamine, suggesting the involvement of the reward system, and of norepinephrine, which they suggest reflects attentional processes. However, there were no differences in the levels of 5-HT in the CSF of gamblers and controls, suggesting that gambling is not physiologically related to compulsive disorders, which do seem to show elevated 5-HT activity.

It seems clear from much that has gone before in this chapter that the production of pleasurable consequences is an essential characteristic of addiction. But, clearly, it is not sufficient to say that pleasure is the basis of addiction. Pleasurable behaviours are not all addictive, or at least not all equally addictive. Perhaps addiction requires the combination of pleasure to produce the addiction and avoidance of withdrawal to maintain it? Alternatively, can we demonstrate that drug addiction and addictive behaviours have the same neural basis? I have pointed out that the neural circuits that are the site of drug addiction are those circuits most believe to be responsible for the reinforcement of behaviour, and hence of much learning. If this is so, then all behaviour with pleasurable consequences must stimulate these circuits. Addictive drugs have the most direct action because they attach to receptors in the circuits or otherwise directly affect biochemical processes there. Some other behaviours to which people are described as becoming addicted, for example exercise, are known to increase the body's production of endorphins, the neurotransmitters whose receptors are stimulated by opiates. The extent to which a behaviour promotes the production of endorphins could well be related to the likelihood of addiction. It has been shown that addicted gamblers have unusually low levels of circulating endorphins, so that gambling is a way in which they can relieve this deficit.

We are, as yet, a long way from being able to provide a satisfactory account of all aspects of addiction. It seems clear that mesolimbic dopaminergic circuits are the core of the addiction, but a full account will need to explain how this is affected by genetic factors, and how personality, social and cultural factors interact to produce addiction.

Summary

Psychoactive drugs, especially caffeine and alcohol, are very widely used. Prolonged use of a particular drug leads to metabolic and functional tolerance. Functional tolerance, the basis of most tolerance to psychoactive drugs, involves changes in receptors at the drug's sites of action and is subject to learning effects; there is also contingent drug tolerance, when tolerance depends on experiencing the effects of the drug, and situational specificity, when tolerance depends on the environmental stimuli associated with taking the drug. The latter can lead to overdose if a drug is taken in an unaccustomed location. Drug tolerance leads to withdrawal symptoms; opposite effects caused by compensatory changes built up during the development of tolerance. Drug dependence is an inability to function normally without the drug. It is possible to be dependent and not addicted (as in many therapeutic situations), and addicted without being dependent (which occurs with cocaine). The physical dependence theory of addiction attributes the condition to the avoidance of the negative consequences of withdrawal which follows from dependence. This is not an adequate explanation as addiction and dependence are not identical and gradual weaning off a drug, eliminating withdrawal symptoms, does not prevent frequent relapse. The positive incentive theory states that people are addicted to the rewarding properties of drugs and that this is mediated by reward mechanisms in the mesolimbic dopamine system of the brain. All addictive drugs act to increase dopamine concentration in this system, either directly or indirectly. The positive incentive theory needs to be combined with an avoidance principle to give a better account of addiction. Genetic, personality and socio-cultural factors all influence drug use and the likelihood of addiction. It is not clear whether gambling and other non-chemical 'addictions' are based on the same mechanisms as drug addiction. There are parallels, but also differences between them.

Further reading

Feldman, R. S., Meyer, J. S. and Quenzer, L. F. (1997) *Principles of Neuropsychopharmacology*, Sunderland, MA: Sinauer Associates. This provides an authoritative survey of the effects of drugs on psychological functions, and the underlying mechanisms of their action.

Ghodse, H. (1995) *Drugs and Addictive Behaviour: A Guide to Treatment*, second edition, London: Blackwell Science. This book is oriented towards clinical issues, but provides a good discussion of definitions and theoretical issues, as well as detailing the effects of different classes of drug and looking at the psychosocial effects of drug use.

McMurran, M. (1994) *The Psychology of Addiction*, London: Taylor and Francis. This highly accessible book concentrates on non-biological (that is social, psychological and emotional) aspects of addiction including behavioural (non-substance) addiction.

Chapter 9

Cognitive and social motives

M OST PEOPLE READING THE preceding chapters will agree that they fall far short of giving a convincing account of motivated human behaviour. Even if we argue that human actions are ultimately, like those of other species, driven by an underlying need to increase the representation of our genes in succeeding generations, this is not a satisfactory explanation for day-to-day human behaviour. Nor are most likely to be convinced that what seem to be specifically human motives are derived by simple learning principles from the biological motives that we have looked at. In preceding chapters we have seen some of the effects of learning and culture that influence our satisfaction of the basic drives. In this chapter we will look briefly at motives that have been considered to be more characteristic of humans than of other species.

The motives we will be looking at in this chapter may be called cognitive and social motives. Most of the research on these motives has been conducted within the framework of social psychology rather than of physiological psychology. While the use of physiological concepts is as widespread in social as in other areas of psychology (Wagner, 1988), it is outside the scope of this book to consider social motives in any detail. I will concern myself largely with their biological significance and continuity. The chapter will close with a short overview of the role of psycho-biological explanations of motivation.

Curiosity

One type of motivation, which we could call cognitive and which is common to humans and other animals, is curiosity. Animals will usually explore a novel environment. Monkeys, for example, will repeatedly open a catch without any external reward, and will work to open a window of a closed cage with no reward other

COGNITIVE AND SOCIAL MOTIVES

than the view. It would be simple to say that there is a basic curiosity drive which needs to be satisfied in the same way that there is a hunger drive. However, it has been argued that, unlike drive-reduction motives like hunger, curiosity-driven behaviour does not satiate. That is, the drive seems not to be reduced when the 'consummatory behaviour' of exploration takes place. This would present a problem for drive-reduction theories of this sort of behaviour; if there is a drive for exploration then it should be reduced when exploration takes place.

However, we saw in an earlier chapter that satiation of drives can be, at least partly, stimulus-specific. That is, consummatory behaviour is recommenced when a new stimulus object is offered to the animal or person (sensory-specific satiety, see Chapter 5). The same thing happens with curiosity. A rat, for example, will explore a maze with no external reward but will soon stop doing so when it becomes familiar with it. In the same way humans become bored when the novelty of a new situation wears off. However, put the rat in a new maze, or give the person something new to think about, and exploratory behaviour or interest is rekindled. What *is* different about this is that there appears to be no longer term satiety. We cannot go on introducing new food indefinitely; eventually general satiety occurs. This does not appear to be the case with curiosity.

Biologically this makes sense. The needs underlying most of the other biological drives are ones that can be satisfied episodically and may satisfy specific tissue deficits. Curiosity might be based on a need to be aware of the environment so as to be able to respond efficiently, for example to threat. So, whenever an aspect of the environment changes it needs to be explored. This same is true of defensive aggression. The animal needs to be able to respond whenever it, or its status, is attacked and, like curiosity, aggression does not satiate.

Optimal arousal

In the 1950s a number of theorists, for example Hebb (1955), put forward the view that there is an *optimal level of arousal* for the performance of any activity, and that we actively seek to maintain that level of arousal. If our arousal level falls below the optimum, we experience boredom with the existing situation, and increased interest in different stimuli, seeking novelty or other types of stimulation that will increase arousal. This might be the basis of the curiosity motive. If, on the other hand, arousal level rises above the optimum then we experience anxiety and distress and will engage in activities that reduce arousal. The important distinction between the optimal arousal approach and the drive approach that we have looked at previously is that in drive-reduction theory consummatory behaviour always reduces drive which, as we saw in Chapter 1, has been conceptualised as a state of heightened arousal.

Drive-reduction theory predicts a linear relation between motivation and performance (see Figure 9.1a). In contrast, one consequence of the optimal arousal view of motivation is that high levels of motivation may actually *disrupt* behaviour, if the associated arousal is above the optimum for that behaviour. Super-optimal arousal is supposed to be the common mechanism by which such states as anxiety, or external conditions such as heat or noise produce a deterioration in performance. This effect is shown in the 'inverted-U' curve that relates performance to

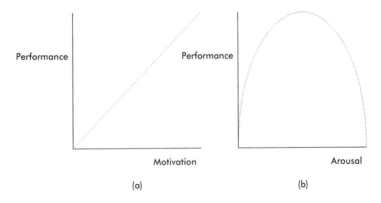

(a) (b)

FIGURE 9.1 (a) Linear relation of motivation and performance according to learning theory. (b) Inverted 'U' relation of arousal and performance

arousal (see Figure 9.1b). The more complex the task to be performed, the lower is the optimal level of arousal, a relationship often glorified with the name Yerkes–Dodson Law. Higher levels of arousal produce disorganisation of behaviour by, it is hypothesised, promoting the performance of dominant responses when a choice is required amongst competing responses. More complex tasks have more competing responses so that their optimal arousal level is lower.

Curiosity-driven behaviour, then, was viewed by arousal theorists as an attempt to raise sub-optimal levels of arousal, which would be experienced as aversive (e.g. boredom). The clearest example of this comes from studies of sensory deprivation in which a subject is put into a chamber in which stimulation is reduced to a minimum. This is found to be a very unpleasant experience, and subjects frequently request early release from the experiment (see Solomon *et al.*, 1961). From the point of view of arousal theory this suggests that the subjects have a need for stimulation because of their sub-optimal arousal. But this is not a convincing explanation of the curiosity motive. The optimal level of arousal for doing nothing would be expected to be minimal so subjects in sensory deprivation studies should be quite content. Clearly, some other type of explanation is necessary for exploratory behaviour and curiosity.

In an attempt to bring exploratory behaviour and other aspects of the apparent drive for optimal arousal under the same drive-reduction framework as other forms of motivation, Berlyne (1960) proposed that we always seek to reduce our level of arousal to the *minimum* possible, so that the optimal level is actually zero. The apparent contradiction with the inverted-U phenomenon comes about because we find both environments that are too simple and those that are too complex to be highly arousing, and hence aversive. This is illustrated by the fact that sensory deprivation is not only unpleasant but is accompanied by autonomic manifestations of arousal. The aim of motivated behaviour, then, is not to seek an optimal level of arousal, but to seek situations that provide the minimum of arousal and such situations are moderate in complexity and novelty.

Self-integrative motives

Much human motivation has been described as self-integrative; that is, there are motives aimed at regulating self-perception and self-esteem. The individual is described as having *needs* related to understanding, mastery, self-actualisation, achievement and cognitive consistency. Cognitive consistency motives will be dealt with in the next section. In this section we will look at another self-integrative motive, achievement motivation, that has received a great deal of research attention. However, while this has been an extremely influential approach in social psychology, there is little we can say about it from a psychobiological view, so I shall not devote much space to it.

Achievement motivation

Need for achievement was the most intensively studied of the self-integrative motives in the 1950s to 1970s. It was proposed by Murray in 1938 as a universal and important human motive. McClelland and Atkinson and their colleagues launched a research programme in the 1950s into the need to achieve, which they defined as a need for success in gaining a standard of excellence (McClelland *et al.*, 1953). Early investigations of achievement motivation used a **projective test** known as the *Thematic Apperception Test* (TAT) in which a person is shown ambiguous pictures and asked to tell stories about what the pictures represent. The individual's motivation is reflected in the themes that emerge in the interpretation of the stories. Thus, hungry people tend to produce stories containing food themes, and the stories of people who had been led to believe that they had failed tests of leadership qualities contain themes related to performance and goal attainment. Such themes were interpreted as indicating that these people had an elevated need for achievement following their perceived failure in the leadership tests.

The theory of achievement motivation was developed independently by Atkinson and McClelland over the course of the following 20 years or so. Atkinson linked the mechanism of achievement motivation closely to emotional outcomes of situations (see, for example, Atkinson, 1964). The person experiences a conflict between approach and avoidance tendencies when faced with a challenge. Attempting the challenge results in conflicting emotions: *positive affective anticipations*, notably of pride, if the challenge is successfully met; and *negative affective anticipations*, such as shame, if the attempt fails. This leads to approach–avoidance dilemma; a hope of success balanced against a fear of failure. A person's tendency to take on the challenge (approach) is determined by the combination of the person's need for achievement, the perceived probability of success and the incentive value (reward) of success. The avoidance tendency, similarly, results from the person's fear of failure, the perceived probability of failure and the negative incentive value of failure (how much shame would be experienced). The person's behaviour faced with a challenge is determined by the difference in the strength of the tendency to approach and the tendency to avoid the situation.

From a biological point of view, achievement motivation may be one way in which individuals achieve status and power, akin to the continual struggle to rise up the 'pecking order' in other species.

Cognitive consistency

During the late 1950s and the 1960s, another prominent approach was to argue that a major source of human motivation is the need to maintain consistency amongst our cognitions (beliefs, attitudes, feelings and knowledge). The most widely discussed of these theories of cognitive consistency was the *cognitive dissonance theory* of Festinger (1957). Basically, this proposed that whenever people experience a mismatch amongst their cognitions they experience a state of dissonance. Dissonance is motivating, producing behaviour that reduces the mismatch, and hence the dissonance. The motivation need not result in overt acts but can lead to changes in cognitions. For example, smokers presented with evidence that smoking is injurious to health are put into a state of dissonance since the two cognitions ('I smoke' and 'smoking is dangerous') are inconsistent. They are therefore motivated to reduce the dissonance. Since the dissonance is between two cognitions, the individual can reduce the dissonance by changing either or both of the cognitions. The strength of the motivation to reduce dissonance is determined by the number of dissonant cognitions, and by their importance to the individual.

A problem with this type of theory is that it does not specify how dissonance will be reduced. Clearly, even if only two cognitions are dissonant, either one could be altered. Cognitive dissonance theory introduced the notion that cognitions differ in their degree of resistance to change. Those that are less resistant to change will be most likely to be changed to reduce dissonance. Thus, for example, the smoker could stop smoking or could change the cognitions about the adverse effects of smoking. Stopping smoking may be very difficult (resistant to change), and it is more likely that the smoker will modify the adverse-effects cognition. For example, they could find reasons not to accept the evidence (e.g. 'it's only correlational or based on research with dogs') or to reduce its relevance to them (e.g. 'I don't have other risk factors'), or they could focus on apparent benefits of smoking (e.g. 'it helps me to relax'). In more complex dissonance situations the factor of resistance to change is unlikely to be sufficient to tell us what type of action or change will occur as a result of the motivation to reduce the dissonance.

Subsequent discussions of cognitive dissonance theory have focused either on the nature of the state of dissonance itself, or on the situations that give rise to dissonance. The state of dissonance has been described as being exactly like a biological drive, associated with increased physiological arousal (e.g. Brehm and Cohen, 1962). However, direct measurement of physiological changes has not always shown that dissonance-inducing situations produce arousal. Further, when arousal is induced it is not necessarily accompanied by cognitive changes or, conversely, when cognitive change occurs it is not accompanied by arousal reduction (see Fazio and Cooper, 1983).

Social motivation

Human behaviour is embedded, implicitly or explicitly, in a social framework. As a consequence of this we should expect not only that it will be influenced by social factors, but also that social interaction provides sources of motivation for the individual. We could identify and label an enormous number of social motives with varying degrees of specificity of goals. In some of the motives we consider in this section we will observe similarities between human behaviour and that of other species. The archaeological evidence shows that human beings evolved to live in groups of up to 50 persons. This is a similar pattern to our closest relatives, the chimpanzees. Given the properties of groups, it is likely that motivational processes will have evolved to promote the functions of the group, ultimately, modern biology insists, to the advantage of the individual.

Social facilitation

The simplest motivational effect of being in a social group was first recorded 100 years ago when Triplett noted that cyclists could ride faster when in direct competition with others than when alone. The concerted study of *social facilitation*, as it became known, followed a review and theoretical analysis by Zajonc (1965). Two features of social facilitation will be mentioned here. First, the effects could be observed in many other species, including chickens, fish and rats. Second, the effect of presence of other members of the same species was not always to enhance performance; sometimes performance deteriorated.

Zajonc's explanation of these effects was that the mere presence of another member of the same species induces a state of arousal which combines with the existing drive state of the animal. As we have seen before, the effect of increasing drive depends on the nature of the behaviour being undertaken. Performance of simple or well-practised tasks is enhanced because higher drive facilitates the emission of correct dominant responses, while that of difficult or new tasks deteriorates due to the facilitation of competing, incorrect behaviours. This drive theory of social presence effects was dominant until the late 1970s, although Zajonc's view that the arousal response is a 'hard-wired' one was challenged by Cottrell (1972), who argued that performance was not affected if the other people present were blindfolded, suggesting a learned origin for the effect.

Alternative conceptions of social facilitation phenomena in humans have more recently been proposed. Guerin (1986) concluded that the effects are related to the subject's *uncertainty* about the actions of others in the situation, while Baron (1986) argued that the effect is one of distraction leading to *cognitive overload*. Each of these views accounts for much of the existing evidence. Baron's view does not depend on the assumption that the effects are mediated by increased arousal.

Self-presentation

Social presence effects have been shown to be greater when the other persons have higher perceived status than the subject (e.g. Seta *et al.*, 1989), and when they are strangers rather than friends (e.g. Wagner and Smith, 1991). This supports the view that the facilitative or disruptive effects of social presence result from a concern with how other people will evaluate one's performance and oneself. This concern, known as *evaluation apprehension*, is one manifestation of a more general motivation to present oneself in as good a light as possible. Social psychologists call self-presentation motivation *impression management*, and have viewed it as a fundamental human motive (Schlenker, 1980). Successful and unsuccessful impression management lead to variations in *self-esteem* and its associated emotions of pride, satisfaction and pleasure, on the one hand, and embarrassment, shame, self-pity and sadness on the other.

Self-presentation can be seen to have its origins in the importance of group membership with its evolutionary origins. Good impression management will promote group membership (social inclusion) while poor impression management will tend to result in social rejection. But it also has elements of competition, and achievement motivation could be a fairly general expression of this.

The competitive aspect of group membership is for many expressed as a need, not just to be a member of a group, but to increase one's status within the group. This could be achieved in any number of ways, partly determined by the society in which the individual lives, for example by the accumulation of possessions, wealth, attractive partners, education, positions of authority and power. Most directly, and in a way most closely parallel to that in other species, it can be achieved by the direct exertion of physical violence.

Cooperation and altruism

Group membership has another implication for the individual and that is cooperation. Like all other behaviour, cooperation works as an evolutionary principle because it promotes the survival of the individual's genes. Usually this is because it makes the individual more likely to survive and pass on its genes to the next generation. But in some exceptional cases, such as the social insects like honey bees, this evolutionary principle cannot operate in this way since most individuals do not, or cannot, reproduce. How does the apparently selfless cooperation amongst the social insects promote the selfish gene? Hamilton (1972) showed that, because of the curious genetic make-up of male bees and ants, who only have half of the usual number of chromosomes, the female workers are more closely related to their fellows (sisters) than they would be to their own offspring if they were to have them. This leads to the evolution of a communal life-style which promotes the reproduction of the sole fertile female (the queen) at the expense of the individual worker. Indirectly, this gives the individual worker's genes the greatest chance of survival in the next generation.

But there is a further interesting aspect of social living. People, and animals, sometimes perform acts which seem to serve the needs of others even if it is to the detriment of themselves. We call such acts altruism. But, 'if you look at the way natural selection works, it seems to follow that anything that has evolved by natural selection should be selfish' (Dawkins, 1976: 4). So, acts of altruism apparently cannot be a part of evolved behaviour. However, in the animal world, what appear to be acts of altruism can always be identified as tending to enhance the chances of survival of the individual animal's own genes. Thus, for example, the bird who puts on a 'broken wing' display to draw a predator away from the bird's nest containing its young has a chance of being killed itself, but at the same time increases the survival chances of the copies of its genes carried by its young in the nest. There are many examples of such altruistic behaviour on the part of parents. Harder to understand at first sight is the behaviour of worker bees who sting in the defence of their colony, following which they die because internal organs are everted along with the sting. An analysis like that given in the previous paragraph shows that this behaviour, like cooperation, is actually in the interests of the survival of genetic material.

Less directly, altruistic behaviour in social groups in other species serves the same selfish function. Trivers (1971) showed that such altruism is *reciprocal* and that it evolved in, essentially, a 'you scratch my back and I'll scratch yours' way. That is, as long as the cost of performing an altruistic behaviour is less than the benefit of receiving it, both the giver and the receiver benefit in the longer term. A typical example is food sharing. If an animal has obtained more food than it can consume in one sitting, it will frequently allow other group members to consume it. This is of little cost to the individual as it has eaten its fill, and in future the individual is likely to be the recipient of such behaviour.

Nowak and Sigmund (1998) have argued that the most general mechanism by which cooperation and altruism have evolved is an *indirect* reciprocity, the benefits of which to the individual are even less obvious. In their view, cooperation and altruism confer an advantage because the individual becomes perceived as a valuable member of the social group and benefits indirectly from being so perceived. So, all altruism in the animal world is essentially selfish.

Humans are also capable of altruistic behaviour and may be said to be driven by altruistic motives. Is this also essentially selfish? Nowak and Sigmund see indirect reciprocity as the crucial step in the evolution of human society. It might seem cynical to say so, but it is possible to construe all human altruism as self-serving even if the pay-off is the prospect of reward in an after-life. On the day-to-day level we may gain pride, satisfaction and status, as well as building up a store of potential reciprocal acts, or indirectly from becoming known as a good citizen, from selfless deeds.

The limits of psychobiology

It is obvious that there is a huge gulf between the physiological drives with which we have been concerned in most of this book, and the types of motivation that we have looked at in this chapter. Yet there are numerous similarities. As we have seen, many of these cognitive and social motives are akin to physiological motives to the extent that they all seem to operate on the basis of needs (be they physiological, cognitive or social) that drive us to satisfy those needs. Underlying many of these drives, it has been hypothesised, are common states of arousal. Arousal energises the motive while internal and/or external cues direct it.

Sociobiology can point to parallels between much human behaviour and that of other species, arguing that much of what we do has its origins in behaviour that serves reproductive goals in other species. But we must be careful not to let these parallels lead us to believe that we thereby *understand* these human behaviours. Human beings have *control* over the satisfaction of our motives, and this is as true of the basic, physiological drives as of cognitive and social motives. We should no more accept that the origins of extra-marital sexual intercourse in improved reproductive success (Baker and Bellis, 1995) explain or justify it, than we should argue that the murder of a child is justified because it, too, has parallels in animal behaviour, for example when a lion taking over a pride kills all the existing young (again with the biological end of reproductive success).

The point is that we are capable of *avoiding* following these biological objectives. Returning to altruism, it is, of course, impossible to decide if human altruism is essentially selfish, or if it has the evolutionary significance suggested for that of other species. As Dawkins put it, 'It is possible that yet another unique quality of man is a capacity for genuine, disinterested, true altruism. I hope so ...' (1976: 215).

Summary

Curiosity is a widespread 'cognitive' motive that is presumably based on a biological need to be familiar with the environment so as to be able to respond to emergencies most efficiently. A proposed physiological basis for curiosity is the requirement for maintaining a certain level of arousal. If arousal is too low then stimulation is sought, at the simplest level by exploration of the surroundings. Achievement motivation is a self-integrative motive. It has not been studied from a psychobiological perspective, although it could be argued that it is a human expression of the competitiveness that forms social hierarchies in other species. Cognitive dissonance theory argues that we have a basic drive to maintain consistency amongst our beliefs, attitudes and behaviour. Inconsistencies are held to lead to a state of drive, equated with arousal, which has to be reduced by reducing the dissonance. The mere presence of others has motivational consequences. This, too, has been explained by increased arousal interacting with the complexity of the task to be performed, either enhancing or disrupting performance. Some effects of social presence are explained by a need to present oneself in the best possible light, and may also be ascribed a biological origin in status hierarchies. Cooperation is widespread amongst other species and apparent altruism also occurs. It can always be shown that these acts serve the general principle of the enhanced survival of the individual's genes. Whether or not this applies to human altruism it is impossible to decide.

Further reading

Ridley, M. (1996) *The Origins of Virtue*, Harmondsworth: Penguin Books. Matt Ridley displays a rare combination of scholarship and ability for entertaining writing to provide an account of the way in which cooperation and the division of labour amongst group members have evolved.

Weiner, B. (1992) *Human Motivation: Metaphors, Theory and Research*, London: Sage. Weiner has long been a respected writer on motivation. This is a scholarly review of the field.

Glossary

The first occurrence of each of these terms is high-lighted in **bold** type in the main text.

5-HT 5-hydroxytryptamine *See* **serotonin.**

acetylcholine A widely distributed neurotransmitter.

ACTH *See* **adrenocorticotropic hormone.**

action potential The electrical impulse that carries information along an axon.

activating effect of hormones A reversible behavioural effect of a hormone.

addiction A state characterised by an overwhelming involvement with the use of a drug, or with other behaviour, and a high tendency to relapse into that behaviour after stopping.

ADH *See* **antidiuretic hormone.**

adipose tissues Tissues composed of fat cells which are the body's main long-term energy store.

adrenal cortex The outer layer of the adrenal gland secreting glucocorticoid, mineralocorticoid and androgen hormones.

adrenal medulla The inner part of the adrenal gland secreting mainly epinephrine.

adrenocorticotropic hormone An anterior pituitary hormone controlling secretions of the adrenal cortex.

adrenogenital syndrome Any one of a number of genetic disorders that cause excessive secretion of androgens in females.

afferent Carrying sensory information towards the central nervous system, hence afferent neurone, afferent signal.

aldosterone An adrenal cortical hormone causing salt retention by kidneys.

AMH *See* **anti-Müllerian hormone.**

amino acids Substances that are the building blocks of proteins.

amygdala A group of nuclei in the cerebral hemispheres involved in processing of motivationally related sensory information.

androgen insensitivity syndrome A genetic disorder involving insensitivity of androgen receptors, causing an XY foetus to develop with external female genitalia.

androgens A group of male sex hormones, including testosterone.

angiotensin A hormone produced in the blood which leads to constriction of blood vessels, the secretion of aldosterone and thirst.

anorexia nervosa A life-threatening condition involving extreme concern with body weight and self-starvation.

ANS *See* **autonomic nervous system.**

anterior commissure A fibre bundle connecting parts of the cerebral hemispheres.

antidiuretic hormone Posterior pituitary hormone that controls water secretion by the kidneys and acts as a central neurotransmitter.

anti-Müllerian hormone A hormone produced by the testes of a male foetus which prevents the Müllerian ducts from developing into internal female genitalia.

aphagia Failure to eat.

autonomic nervous system That part of the nervous system concerned with automatic control of internal organs.

axon The extension of a neurone that carries the action potential.

baroreceptor A receptor for blood pressure found in the heart and major blood vessels.

basic rest–activity cycle The 90-minute cycle underlying variations in alertness and the SW–REM sleep cycle.

behaviourist Relating to the school of psychology that focused on overt behaviours as responses to external stimuli, rather than on mental states or processes.

blood-brain barrier The lower permeability of blood capillaries in the brain, protecting the brain from blood-borne chemicals.

BRAC *See* **basic rest–activity cycle.**

brain stem The brain region consisting of the midbrain, the pons and the medulla.

capillaries The smallest blood vessels through the walls of which substances pass between the blood and other tissues.

CCK *See* **cholecystokinin.**

cell membrane The complex outer layer of a cell which contains receptors for chemical messengers.

central nervous system That part of the nervous system comprising the brain and spinal cord.

cerebral cortex The outer layer of the cerebral hemispheres consisting of densely packed neurones.

cerebral hemisphere One of the two (left and right) halves of the forebrain.

cerebral ventricle One of the fluid-filled chambers within the brain.

cerebrospinal fluid The liquid filling the cerebral ventricles and surrounding the brain.

cholecystokinin A hormone secreted by the gut that acts peripherally and centrally as a satiety signal.

chromosome A strand of DNA and supporting proteins found in the nucleus of cells and which carries genetic information.

circadian rhythm Any cyclical variation of activity (behavioural and physiological) that has a period of about one day.

circannual rhythm Any biological rhythm with a period of about one year.

circumventricular organs A number of neural centres adjacent to the cerebral ventricles and outside the blood–brain barrier.

clone An organism (or DNA) produced asexually that is genetically identical to another organism (or DNA).

CNS *See* **central nervous system.**

conditioned aversion The learned avoidance of particular foods following their association with aversive consequences such as nausea or illness.

contingent drug tolerance Tolerance to the effects of a drug that depends on experiencing those effects.

corpus callosum The main fibre bundle connecting the two cerebral hemispheres.

corpus luteum An ovarian body that develops from a follicle after ovulation and which secretes oestradiol and progesterone.

corticosteroids A class of steroid hormones produced by the adrenal cortex.

corticotropin releasing hormone A hypothalamic hormone that causes the anterior pituitary to secrete adrenocorticotropic hormone. (Also known as corticotropin releasing factor.)

cortisol The main glucocorticoid hormone of the adrenal cortex, involved in regulation of metabolism.

CRH *See* **corticotropin releasing hormone.**

CSF *See* **cerebrospinal fluid.**

defeminising effect Any manipulation or change (such as prevention of oestrogen activity) that causes structures or behaviour to be less feminine.

defensive aggression Aggressive behaviour in response to an attack.

demasculinising effect Any manipulation or change (such as prevention of androgen activity) that causes structures or behaviour to be less masculine.

deoxyribonucleic acid The complex molecule that carries genetic information.

depolarisation A reduction in the membrane potential of a cell, particularly a neurone, increasing the probability of an action potential starting.

detoxification A treatment for drug addiction (especially alcoholism) based on the gradual withdrawal of the drug.

diurnal Being active during daylight hours.

dizygotic twins Twins born from two fertilised ova, hence no more similar genetically than any pair of siblings.

DNA *See* **deoxyribonucleic acid.**

dominance hierarchy The pecking order in any group of animals of the same species.

dopamine A central nervous system neurotransmitter involved in central reward circuits.

drive A motive or the energy by which a motive is driven.

drive-reduction theory An explanation of motivation based on the notion that consummatory behaviour meets an underlying need, reducing the motivation for that behaviour.

drug dependence A state in which an individual requires a drug in order to function normally.

drug tolerance Decreased sensitivity to the effects of a drug following repeated administration.

ectotherm An animal that is unable to control its body temperature homeostatically.

EEG *See* **electroencephalogram (-graph).**

efferent Carrying commands from the central nervous system to effector organs and muscles, hence efferent neurone, efferent signal.

electroencephalogram (-**graph**) A recording (or the equipment on which it is made) of the electrical activity of the brain, made using electrodes placed on the scalp.

electrolyte A substance which, when dissolved in water (or the resulting solution), carries an electrical current.

endocrine gland A gland whose function is to secrete hormones.

endometrium The vascular lining of the uterus which builds up during the menstrual cycle, breaking down at menstruation.

endorphins A group of naturally occurring opioids.

endothermy Having the ability to control body temperature through homeostasis.

enzyme A chemical that controls a specific chemical reaction, for example speeding the breakdown of neurotransmitters.

epinephrine The hormone produced by the adrenal medulla, and which acts as a CNS neurotransmitter.

feminising effect A consequence of a natural or induced change (such as removal of perinatal androgens) that renders the animal structurally or behaviourally more feminine.

follicle-stimulating hormone An anterior pituitary hormone that causes the development of the ovarian follicle or promotes the production of sperm.

follicular phase That part of the menstrual cycle between the end of menstruation and the release of an ovum by the follicle.

forebrain The brain region comprising the cerebral hemispheres, amygdala, corpus callosum and hippocampus.

free-running rhythm The circadian rhythm that emerges when an animal is kept isolated from external cues.

FSH *See* **follicle stimulating hormone.**

functional tolerance Tolerance to a drug resulting from a reduction in reactivity of the sites of action, caused by changes in the structure or number of receptor sites, or changes in the structure of cell membranes.

GABA Gamma-aminobutyric acid, a central neurotransmitter, usually inhibitory.

ganglion A neural centre outside the CNS, notably in the sympathetic nervous system.

genes The units of genetic information carrying instructions for the synthesis of a particular chemical substance.

genotype The genetic make-up of an organism (as distinct from **pheno-type**).

glucagon A pancreatic hormone causing the release of stored energy into the blood.

glucocorticoids A class of adrenal cortical hormones involved in regulating metabolism.

glucoreceptors Neurones sensitive to the concentration of glucose in the blood.

glutamate A widespread excitatory neurotransmitter in the central nervous system.

glycogen A complex carbohydrate, the form in which glucose is stored.

GnRH *See* **gonadotropin-releasing hormone.**

gonadotropic hormones Anterior pituitary hormones acting on the gonads (including luteinising hormone and follicle-stimulating hormone).

gonadotropin-releasing hormone A hypothalamic hormone causing the anterior pituitary to secrete gonadotropic hormones.

habituation Non-associative learning causing a decrease in response to a continued or repeated stimulus.

hindbrain The region of the brain consisting of the pons, the medulla and the cerebellum.

homeostasis The automatic physiological processes, based on negative feedback loops, by which the body's internal environment is controlled.

homeostatic behaviour Behaviour which promotes homeostasis.

HY antigen A substance produced by a gene on the Y chromosome which causes the gonads of a male foetus to develop into testes.

hyperphagia Over-eating, particularly as a result of lesions in the ventro-medial hypothalamus.

hypertonic Of a solution, having a greater concentration of a solute than a neighbouring solution, from which it will draw water through a semi-permeable membrane.

hypothalamus A forebrain structure lying immediately beneath the thalamus, containing numerous nuclei important in autonomic control and motivation.

hypotonic Of a solution, having a lower concentration than a neighbouring solution, to which it will lose water through a semi-permeable membrane.

INAH-3 *See* **third interstitial nucleus of the anterior hypothalamus.**

infradian rhythm Any biological rhythm with a frequency less than daily, for example the menstrual cycle.

insulin A pancreatic hormone that promotes the storage of glucose as glycogen, and fats in adipose tissue.

interstitial fluid The liquid filling the spaces between cells.

intracellular fluid The liquid contained within cells.

ion A charged atom or molecule.

isotonic Of solutions, having the same concentration of solutes so that water will not pass between them.

lipids Fats and related substances, including fatty acids and cholesterol.

lordosis The sexually receptive position adopted by female rodents.

luteal phase The part of the menstrual cycle from ovulation until menstruation.

luteinising hormone A gonadotropic hormone released by the anterior hypothalamus, promoting either ovulation or sperm and testosterone production.

LutH *See* **luteinising hormone.**

macronutrients The three main food groups, proteins, carbohydrates and fats.

masculinising effect Any natural or induced change that causes structures or behaviour to be more masculine.

MDS *See* mesolimbic dopamine system.

median preoptic nucleus A nucleus close to the circumventricular organs which is involved in the control of drinking.

medulla The medulla oblongata, part of the hindbrain channelling internal sensations (including taste) and involved in arousal.

melatonin A hormone secreted by the pineal gland in response to darkness. In humans probably concerned with synchronising external and endogenous rhythms.

mesolimbic dopamine system A network of dopaminergic neurones extending from the ventral tegmental area to basal forebrain areas, and thought to be involved in reinforcement and addiction.

metabolic tolerance Drug tolerance resulting from increased rate of metabolism of drugs.

microsleeps Very brief occurrences of sleep, occurring especially in sleep-deprived persons.

midbrain A brain region between the pons and forebrain structures containing centres involved in many motivated behaviours.

mineralocorticoids A group of steroid hormones secreted by the adrenal cortex involved in water and electrolyte balance.

monozygotic twins Twins resulting from the division of a single fertilised ovum and therefore with identical genotypes.

MPN *See* **median preoptic nucleus.**

Müllerian ducts Undifferentiated foetal structures that develop into the internal female genitalia.

natural selection The evolutionary process by which an individual with a genetically determined advantage has an increased likelihood of passing that advantage on to succeeding generations.

negative feedback The key aspect of a self-modulated control system.

neocortex The most recently evolved area of the brain concerned with sensory awareness and voluntary control of movement.

neurone A nerve cell, the basic functional unit of the nervous system.

neuropeptide Y A neurotransmitter involved in the control of feeding.

neurotransmitter A chemical substance produced by axon terminals of a pre-synaptic neurone which attaches to receptors in the post-synaptic membrane, altering its polarisation.

nocturnal Active during the night.

norepinephrine A peripheral sympathetic and central nervous system neurotransmitter.

NST *See* **nucleus of the solitary tract.**

nucleus accumbens A basal forebrain centre involved in reinforcement.

nucleus of the solitary tract A centre in the medulla receiving internal sensory information.

oestradiol The main oestrogen hormone.

oestrogens A class of female sex hormones secreted mainly by ovarian follicles.

oestrus cycle The reproductive cycle of female mammals other than primates.

offensive aggression Aggressive behaviour directed usually at a member of the same species.

opioids Naturally occurring peptides that attach to receptors in the brain, producing effects mimicked by exogenous opiates.

organising effect of hormones A permanent structural change produced by a hormone preparing the body for a particular type of behaviour.

organum vasculosum of the lamina terminalis A circumventricular organ containing osmoreceptors, and involved in the control of drinking.

osmoreceptor A neurone sensitive to the concentration of electrolytes in the blood, thereby playing a role in thirst and drinking.

osmosis The movement of water molecules from hypotonic to hypertonic solutions through a membrane.

OVLT *See* **organum vasculosum of the lamina terminalis.**

oxytocin A posterior pituitary hormone involved in lactation and male and female sexual response.

pancreas An endocrine gland in the abdomen secreting insulin and glucagon.

parabrachial nucleus A nucleus in the pons involved in receiving autonomic afferent neurones.

parasympathetic nervous system The branch of the autonomic nervous system controlling resting functions.

paraventricular nucleus A nucleus in the hypothalamus producing posterior pituitary hormones.

peptide A substance consisting of a chain of amino acids.

periaqueductal grey matter A midbrain region organising species-typical behaviours such as feeding and mating (also known as central grey matter).

peribrachial area An area of the pons controlling the onset of REM sleep.

peripheral nervous system The nervous system apart from the brain and spinal cord.

PGO waves Bursts of activity starting in the pons and travelling to visual areas of the brain, seen in REM sleep.

phenotype The organism resulting from the interaction of the genotype and the environment.

pheromone A chemical substance secreted by one animal which communicates with other members of the species.

phylogenetic tree The evolutionary relationships amongst species.

pituitary gland A group of three endocrine glands under the hypothalamus secreting numerous hormones.

PNS *See* **parasympathetic nervous system.**

polarisation The relative ionic state of the fluids across a membrane. Depolarisation initiates the action potential in a neurone.

polygenic Of the genetic determination of a characteristic, indicates that more than one gene is involved.

pons An area of the hindbrain between the medulla and the midbrain.

positive incentive properties The characteristic of a behaviour such as drinking that produces a tendency to continue the behaviour.

postganglionic fibre (neurone) A neurone in the autonomic nervous system that terminates on the effector organs.

precursors Chemically, substances from which a particular active chemical are synthesised in the body.

predation A type of aggression or feeding behaviour involving a single attack on a member of (usually) another species and without overt display.

preganglionic fibre (neurone) A neurone in the autonomic nervous system that has its cell body in the CNS and terminates in the autonomic ganglia.

preoptic area A region of the hypothalamus, different parts of which are involved in slow-wave sleep and in aggression.

proceptive behaviour Behaviour displayed by an animal that indicates its sexual interest to another animal.

progesterone A hormone produced by the ovaries that maintains the endometrium and promotes receptivity in appropriate parts of the oestrus cycle.

projective test A diagnostic psychological test which some practitioners use to reveal hidden concerns and motives.

prolactin An anterior pituitary hormone that produces lactation and in the male inhibits sexual activity, for example immediately after ejaculation.

psychoactive drug Any exogenous substance that changes an animal's psychological state.

raphé nuclei A group of nuclei in the brain stem involved in sleep and in drinking.

rapid eye-movement sleep A stage of sleep characterised by a fast EEG and rapid eye-movements, and during which most dream activity occurs.

RAS *See* reticular activating system.

receptive behaviour A species-typical behaviour of a female animal permitting and promoting copulation.

receptor molecule A protein in cell membranes that is receptive to a specific messenger molecule (neurotransmitter or hormone).

REM sleep *See* rapid eye-movement sleep.

renin A hormone secreted by the kidneys in response to increased blood flow and which causes the production of angiotensin in the blood.

reticular activating system A network of neurones in the brain stem that maintains the level of activation of higher and lower neural centres.

reticular formation A network of neurones in the brain stem involved in maintaining the arousal of the brain and spinal cord.

satiety centre A putative centre in the brain signalling the satisfaction of a need for food or water.

SCN *See* suprachiasmatic nucleus.

SDN *See* sexually dimorphic nucleus.

selfish gene The view that animal (and human) behaviour has evolved to increase the probability of an individual's genes being passed on to succeeding generations.

semipermeable membrane A membrane, such as those of animal cells, permitting the passage of some, but not all, molecules.

sensory-specific satiety Satiety for a specific food without general satiety.

serotonin A central neurotransmitter.

set point The value of a system variable that is maintained by negative feedback control systems underlying motivation and homeostasis.

sexual dimorphism Male–female differences in structure and behaviour.

sexually dimorphic nucleus A nucleus in the preoptic area that is larger in males than in females and which is involved in male sexual behaviour.

SFO *See* **subfornical organ.**

sham feeding Feeding by an animal with a surgical fistula preventing food from reaching, or remaining in, the stomach.

situational specificity of drug tolerance Tolerance to the effects of a drug that is dependent on external cues (such as a usual place of administration).

SNS *See* **sympathetic nervous system.**

sociobiology The application of evolutionary principles to the study of social, and particularly reproductive, behaviour.

solute A chemical substance that is dissolved in water.

somatic nervous system That part of the nervous system concerned with the control of the voluntary (skeletal) muscles.

subfornical organ A circumventricular organ containing neurones sensitive to angiotensin, and involved in the control of drinking.

suprachiasmatic nucleus A hypothalamic nucleus immediately above the optic chiasma which is the location of circadian clocks.

supraoptic nucleus A hypothalamic nucleus synthesising vasopressin and transporting it to the posterior pituitary.

sympathetic nervous system The branch of the autonomic nervous system concerned with the control of emergency changes.

synapse The structure through which most communication between neurones takes place, using chemical transmitters.

synaptic cleft The gap between two neurones involved in a synapse.

synaptic vesicles The mobile structures within neurones in which neurotransmitters are conveyed to the synaptic cleft.

terminal buttons The swollen ends of axon terminals that border the synaptic cleft.

testosterone The main androgen hormone produced mostly in the testes.

thalamus The area of the brain around the third ventricle containing sensory relay centres.

third interstitial nucleus of the anterior hypothalamus A sexually dimorphic nucleus in the hypothalamus.

ultradian rhythm A biological rhythm with a frequency greater than daily, for example the BRAC.

vagus nerve The nerve carrying parasympathetic efferents to the heart and other organs, and afferents from abdominal organs to the brainstem.

vasoconstriction Narrowing of blood vessels.

vasopressin A posterior pituitary hormone that controls water excretion by the kidneys and acts as a central neurotransmitter. (Also called antidiuretic hormone, ADH.)

ventral tegmental area A midbrain area involved in reinforcement.

ventromedial hypothalamus An area of the hypothalamus involved in the control of eating.

VMH *See* ventromedial hypothalamus.

vomeronasal organ A sensory organ in the nose which contains receptors for pheromones.

withdrawal symptoms The adverse effects of stopping taking a drug to which tolerance has built up.

Wolffian ducts Undifferentiated organs in the foetus which, under the influence of testosterone, develop into the male internal genitalia.

Zeitgeber An environmental stimulus that entrains circadian rhythms. Literally 'time-giver'.

zona incerta Part of the midbrain reticular formation involved in drinking behaviour.

References

Adams, D. B. (1986) 'Defense and territorial behavior dissociated by hypothalamic lesions in the rat', *Nature*, 232: 573–4.

Albert, D. J., Dyson, E. M., Petrovic, D. M. and Walsh, M. L. (1988) 'Cohabitation with a female activates testosterone-dependent social aggression in male rats independently of changes in serum testosterone concentration', *Physiology and Behavior*, 44: 9–13.

Albert, D. J., Petrovic, D. M. and Walsh, M. L. (1989) 'Competitive experience activates testosterone-dependent social aggression toward unfamiliar males', *Physiology and Behavior*, 45: 723–7.

Alexander, G. M. and Sherwin, B. B. (1993) 'Sex steroids, sexual behavior, and selection attention for erotic stimuli in women using oral contraceptives', *Psychoneuroendocrinology*, 18: 91–102.

Alexander, G. M., Swerdloff, R. S., Wang, C., Davidson, T., McDonald, V., Steiner, B. and

Hine, M. (1997) 'Androgen-behavior correlation in hypogonadal men and eugonadal men', *Hormones and Behavior*, 31: 110–19.

Alexander, J. E. and Sufka, K. J. (1993) 'Cerebral lateralization in homosexual males: a preliminary EEG investigation', *International Journal of Psychophysiology*, 15: 269–74.

Allen, L. S. and Gorski, R. A. (1992) 'Sexual orientation and the size of the anterior commissure in the human brain', *Proceedings of the National Academy of Science*, 89: 7199–202.

Anand, B. K. and Brobeck, J. R. (1951) 'Localization of a "feeding center" in the hypothalamus of the rat', *Proceedings of the Society for Experimental Biology and Medicine*, 77: 273–5.

Andersson, B. (1953) 'The effect of injections of hypertonic NaCl solutions in different parts of the hypothalamus of goats', *Acta Physiologica Scandinavica*, 28: 188–201.

Andrews, K. M., McGowan, M. K., Gallitano, A. and Grossman, S. P. (1992) 'Water intake during chronic preoptic infusions of osmotically active or inert solutions', *Physiology and Behavior*, 52: 241–5.

Aschoff, J. (1994) 'Naps as integral parts of the wake time within the sleep/wake cycle', *Journal of Biological Rhythms*, 9: 145–55.

Atkinson, J. W. (1964) *An Introduction to Motivation*, Princeton, NJ: Van Nostrand.

Bailey, J. M. and Pillard, R. C. (1991) 'A genetic study of male sexual orientation', *Archives of General Psychiatry*, 48: 1089–96.

Baker, R. R. and Bellis, M. A. (1995) *Human Sperm Competition: Copulation, Masturbation and Infidelity*, London: Chapman and Hall.

Bancroft, J., Sherwin, B., Alexander, G., Davidson, D. and Walker, A. E. (1991) 'Oral contraceptives, androgens and the sexuality of young women. II. The role of androgens', *Archives of Sexual Behavior*, 20: 121–35.

Baron, R. S. (1986) 'Distraction–conflict theory: progress and problems', in L. Berkowitz (ed.) *Advances in Experimental Social Psychology*, Vol. 19, New York: Academic Press.

Bartness, T. J., Powers, J. B., Hastings, M. H., Bittman, E. L. and Goldman, B. D. (1993) 'The timed infusion paradigm for melatonin delivery: What has it taught us about the melatonin signal, its reception, and the photoperiodic control of seasonal response?', *Journal of Pineal Research*, 15: 161–90.

Beauchamp, G. K. and Cowart, B. J. (1993) 'Preferences for high salt concentration among children', *Developmental Psychology*, 26: 539–45.

Bellis, M. A. and Baker, R. R. (1990) 'Do females promote sperm competition: data for humans', *Animal Behavior*, 40: 997–9.

Bem, D. J. (1996) 'Exotic becomes erotic: a developmental theory of sexual orientation', *Psychological Review*, 103: 320–35.

Bergh, C., Eklund, T., Södersten, P. and Nordin, C. (1997) 'Altered dopamine function in pathological gambling', *Psychological Medicine*, 27: 473–5.

Berlyne, D. E. (1960) *Conflict, Arousal, and Curiosity*, New York: McGraw-Hill.

Bernardis, L. L. and Bellinger, L. L. (1996) 'The lateral hypothalamic area revisited: ingestive behavior', *Neuroscience and Biobehavioral Reviews*, 20: 189–287.

Bernstein, I. L. (1981) 'Meal patterns in "free-running humans"', *Physiology and Behavior*, 27: 621–4.

Birch, L. L. and Fisher, J. A. (1996) 'The role of experience in the development of children's eating behavior', in E. D. Capaldi (ed.) *Why We Eat What We Eat*, Washington, DC: American Psychological Association.

Bishop, K. M. and Wahlstein, D. (1997) 'Sex differences in the human corpus callosum: myth or reality?', *Neuroscience and Biobehavioral Reviews*, 21: 581–601.

Bloch, G. J. and Gorski, R. A. (1988) 'Cytoarchitechtonic analysis of the SDN-POA of the intact and gonadectomised rat', *Journal of Comparative Neurology*, 275: 604–12.

Booth, D. A. (1991) 'Influences on human food consumption', in D. J. Ramsay and D. A. Booth (eds) *Thirst: Physiological and Psychological Aspects*, London: Springer-Verlag.

Boulos, Z., Campbell, S. S., Lewy, A. J., Terman, M., Dijk, D. J. and Eastman, C. I. (1995) 'Light treatment for sleep disorders: Consensus report. 7: Jet-lag', *Journal of Biological Rhythms*, 10: 167–76.

Bozarth, M. A. and Wise, R. A. (1984) 'Anatomically distinct opiate receptor fields mediate reward and physical dependence', *Science*, 224: 516–7.

Brehm, J. W. and Cohen, A. (1962) *Explorations in Cognitive Dissonance*, New York: John Wiley.

Bremer, J. (1959) *Asexualization: A Follow-up Study of 244 Cases*, New York: Macmillan.

Brownell, K. D., Greenwood, M. R. C., Stellar, E. and Shrager, E. E. (1986) 'The effects of repeated cycles of weight loss and regain in rats', *Physiology and Behavior*, 38: 459–64.

Buggy, J., Hoffman, W. E., Phillips, M. I., Fisher, A. E. and Johnson, A. K. (1979) 'Osmosensitivity of rat third ventricle and interactions with angiotensin', *American Journal of Physiology*, 236: R75–82.

Cabanac, M. (1979) 'Sensory pleasure', *Quarterly Review of Biology*, 54: 1–29.

Capaldi, E. D. (1996a) 'Conditioned food preferences', in E. D. Capaldi (ed.) *Why We Eat What We Eat*, Washington, DC: American Psychological Association.

—— (ed.) (1996b). *Why We Eat What We Eat: The Psychology of Eating*, Washington, DC: American Psychological Association.

Carrive, P., Bandler, R. and Dampney, A. L. (1989) 'Somatic and autonomic integration in the midbrain of the unanesthetized decerebrate cat: a distinctive pattern evoked by excitation of neurones in the subtentorial portion of the midbrain periaqueductal grey', *Brain Research*, 483: 251–8.

Cartwright, R. D. (1989) 'Dreams and their meaning', in M. H. Kryger, T. Roth and W. C. Dement (eds) *Principles and Practice of Sleep Medicine*, Philadelphia, PA: W. B. Saunders.

Chapman, I. M., Goble, E. A., Wittert, G. A., Morley, J. E. and Horowitz, M. (1998) 'Effect of intravenous glucose and exogenous insulin infusions on short-term appetite and food intake', *American Journal of Physiology*, 274: 596–603.

Clark, J. T., Kalra, P. S., Crowley, W. R., and Kalra, S. P. (1984) 'Neuropeptide Y and human pancreatic polypeptide stimulate feeding behavior in rats', *Endocrinology*, 115: 427–9.

Cloninger, C. R. (1987) 'Neurogenetic adaptive mechanisms in alcoholism', *Science*, 236.

Cole, J. L., Berman, N. and Bodner, R. J. (1997) 'Evaluation of chronic opioid receptor antagonist effects upon weight and intake measures in lean and obese Zucker rats', *Peptides*, 18: 1201–7.

Cologer-Clifford, A., Simon, N. G., Lu, S. F. and Smoluk, S. A. (1997) 'Serotonin agonist-induced decreases in intermale aggression are dependent on brain region and receptor subtype', *Pharmacology, Biochemistry and Behavior*, 58: 425–30.

Cottrell, N. B. (1972) 'Social facilitation', in C. G. McClintock (ed.) *Experimental Social Psychology*, New York: Holt, Rinehart and Winston.

Crowell, C. R., Hinson, R. E. and Siegel, S. (1981) 'The role of conditional drug responses in tolerance to the hypothermic effects of ethanol', *Psychopharmacology*, 73: 51–4.

Dabbs, J. M., Frady, R. I., Catt, T. S. and Besch, N. F. (1987) 'Saliva testosterone and criminal violence in young adult prison inmates', *Psychosomatic Medicine*, 49: 174–82.

Dabbs, J. M. and Hargrove, M. F. (1997) 'Age, testosterone, and behavior among female prison inmates', *Psychosomatic Medicine*, 59: 477–80.

Davis, J. D. and Campbell, C. S. (1973) 'Peripheral control of meal size in the rat: Effect of sham feeding on meal size and drinking rate', *Journal of Comparative and Physiological Psychology*, 83: 379–87.

Dawkins, R. (1976) *The Selfish Gene*, Oxford: Oxford University Press.

Deacon, S. and Arendt, J. (1996) 'Adapting to phase shifts. I. An experimental model for jet lag and shift work', *Physiology and Behavior*, 59: 665–73.

Dement, W. C. (1960) 'The effect of dream deprivation', *Science*, 131: 1705–7.

Deutsch, J. A. and Gonzalez, M. F. (1980) 'Gastric nutrient content signals satiety', *Behavioral and Neural Biology*, 30: 113–16.

de Vries, M. W. and Peeters, F. P. M. L. (1997) 'Melatonin as a therapeutic agent in the treatment of sleep disturbance in depression', *Journal of Nervous and Mental Diseases*, 185: 201–2.

Dittman, R. W., Kappes, M. E. and Kappes, M. H. (1992) 'Sexual behavior in adolescent and adult females with congenital adrenal hyperplasia', *Psychoneuroendocrinology*, 17: 153–70.

Dorner, G., Schenck, B., Schmiedel, B. and Ahrens, L. (1983) 'Stressful events in prenatal life of bi- and homosexual men', *Experimental and Clinical Endocrinology*, 81: 83–7.

Drewnowski, A. (1996) 'The behavioral phenotype in human obesity', in E. D. Capaldi (ed.) *Why We Eat What We Eat*, Washington, DC: American Psychological Association.

Drewnowski, A., Krahn, D. D., Demitrack, M. A., Nairn, K. and Gosnell, B. A. (1995) 'Naloxone, an opiate blocker, reduces the consumption of sweet high-fat foods in obese and lean female binge eaters', *American Journal of Clinical Nutrition*, 61: 1206–12.

Eagly, A. H. and Steffen, V. J. (1986) 'Gender and aggressive behavior: a meta-analytic review of the social psychological literature', *Psychological Bulletin*, 100: 309–30.

REFERENCES

Ehrenkranz, J., Bliss, E. and Sheard, M. (1974) 'Plasma testosterone: correlation with aggressive behavior and social dominance in man', *Psychosomatic Medicine*, 36: 469–75.

Ehrhardt, A. A. and Meyer-Bahlberg, H. F. L. (1981) 'Effects of prenatal sex hormones on gender-related behavior', *Science*, 211: 1312–18.

Ellison, G. D. and Flynn, J. P. (1968) 'Organized aggressive behavior in cats after surgical isolation of the hypothalamus', *Archives Italiennes de Biologie*, 106: 1–20.

El Mansari, M., Sakai, K. and Jouvet, M. (1989) 'Unitary characteristics of presumptive cholinergic tegmental neurons during the sleep–waking cycle in freely moving cats', *Experimental Brain Research*, 76: 519–29.

Engell, D. and Hirsch, E. (1991) 'Environmental and sensory modulation of fluid intake in humans', in D. J. Ramsay and D. A. Booth (eds) *Thirst: Physiological and Psychological Aspects*, London: Springer-Verlag.

Fazio, R. H. and Cooper, J. (1983) 'Arousal in the dissonance process', in J. T. Cacioppo and R. E. Petty (eds) *Social Psychophysiology: a Sourcebook*, New York: Guilford, pp. 122–52.

Festinger, L. (1957) *A Theory of Cognitive Dissonance*, Evanston, IL: Row, Peterson.

Fitzsimons, J. T. (1961) 'Drinking by rats depleted of body fluid without increase in osmotic pressure', *Journal of Physiology*, 159: 297–309.

Fitzsimons, J. T. and Moore-Gillon, M. J. (1980) 'Drinking and antidiuresis in response to reductions in venous return in the dog: neural and endocrine mechanisms', *Journal of Physiology*, 308: 403–16.

Floody, O. R. and Pfaff, D. W. (1977) 'Aggressive behavior in female hamsters: the hormonal basis for fluctuations in female aggressiveness correlated with estrus state', *Journal of Comparative and Physiological Psychology*, 91: 443–64.

Freud, S. (1915) *The Interpretation of Dreams*, New York: Macmillan.

—— (1922) *Beyond the Pleasure Principle*, (authorised translation, 2nd edition) London: Hogarth Press/Institute of Psychoanalysis, 1942.

Fujimoto, S., Inui, A., Kiyoto, N. and Seki, W. (1997) 'Increased cholecystokinin and pancreatic polypeptide responses to a fat-rich meal in patients with restrictive but not bulimic anorexia nervosa', *Biological Psychiatry*, 41: 1068–70.

Garcia, J., Hankins, W. G. and Rusiniak, K. W. (1974) 'Behavioral regulation of the *milieu interne* in man and rat', *Science*, 185: 824–31.

Garcia, J. and Koelling, R. A. (1966) 'Relation of cue to consequence in avoidance learning', *Psychonomic Science*, 4: 123–4.

Garcia-Velasco, J. and Mondragon, M. (1991) 'The incidence of the vomeronasal organ in 1000 human subjects and its possible clinical significance', *Journal of Steroid Biochemistry and Molecular Biology*, 39: 561–3.

Gerkema, M. P. and Daan, S. (1985) 'Ultradian rhythms in behavior: the case of the common vole (*Microtus arvalis*)', in H. Schulz and P. Lavie (eds), *Ultradian Rhythms in Physiology and Behavior*, Berlin: Springer-Verlag, pp. 11–32.

Gilbert, R. M. (1991) 'Alcohol- and caffeine-beverage consumption: Causes other than water deficit', in D. J. Ramsay and D. A. Booth (eds) *Thirst: Physiological and Psychological Aspects*, London: Springer-Verlag.

Gonzalez, M. F. and Deutsch, J. A. (1981) 'Vagotomy abolishes cues of satiety produced by gastric distension', *Science*, 212: 1283–4.

Goodwin, D. W. (1979) 'Alcoholism and heredity: a review and hypothesis', *Archives of General Psychiatry*, 36: 57–61.

Goodwin, D. W., Schulsinger, F., Hermansen, L., Guze, S. B. and Winokur, G. A. (1973) 'Alcohol problems in adoptees raised apart from alcoholic biological parents', *Archives of General Psychiatry*, 128: 239–43.

Gordon, I., Lask, B. and Bryant-Waugh, R. (1997) 'Childhood-onset anorexia nervosa: towards identifying a biological substrate', *International Journal of Eating Disorders*, 22: 159–65.

Gorski, R. A., Gordon, J. H., Shryne, J. E. and Southam, A. M. (1978) 'Evidence for a morphological sex difference within the medial preoptic area of the rat brain', *Brain Research*, 148: 333–46.

Greenberg, R. and Pearlman, C. A. (1974) 'Cutting the REM nerve: An approach to the adaptive role of REM sleep', *Perspectives in Biology and Medicine*, 17: 513–21.

Greenberg, R., Pillard, R. and Pearlman, C. (1972) 'The effect of dream (stage REM) deprivation on adaptation to stress', *Psychosomatic Medicine*, 34: 257–62.

Grill, H. J. and Norgren, R. (1978) 'Chronically decerebrate rats demonstrate satiation but not bait shyness', *Science*, 201: 267–9.

Grunt, J. A. and Young, W. C. (1953) 'Consistency of sexual behavior patterns in individual male guinea pigs following castration and androgen therapy', *Journal of Comparative and Physiological Psychology*, 46: 138–44.

Guan, D., Phillips, W. and Green, G. (1996) 'Inhibition of gastric emptying and food intake by exogenous and endogenous CCK: role of capsaicin-sensitive vagal afferent pathway', *Gastroenterology*, 110: A672.

Guerin, B. (1986) 'Mere presence effects in humans: a review', *Journal of Experimental Social Psychology*, 22: 38–77.

Halpern, C. T., Udry, J. R. and Suchindran, C. (1997) 'Testosterone predicts initiation of coitus in adolescent females', *Psychosomatic Medicine*, 59: 161–71.

Hamer, D. H., Hu, S., Magnusson, V. L., Hu, N. and Pattatucci, A. M. L. (1993) 'A linkage between DNA markers on the X chromosome and male sexual orientation', *Science*, 261: 321–7.

Hamilton, W. D. (1972) 'Altruism and related phenomena, mainly in social insects', *Annual Review of Ecology and Systematics*, 3: 193–232.

Harris, G. and Booth, D. A. (1987) 'Infants' preference for salt in food: its dependence upon recent dietary experience', *Journal of Reproductive and Infant Psychology*, 5: 97–104.

Hartmann, E. (1967) *The Biology of Dreaming*, Springfield, IL: Charles C. Thomas.

Hebb, D. O. (1955) 'Drives and the C.N.S. (Conceptual nervous system)', *Psychological Review*, 62: 243–54.

Heimer, L. and Larsson, K. (1966/7) 'Impairment of mating behavior in male rats following lesions in the preoptic-anterior hypothalamic continuum', *Brain Research*, 3: 248–63.

Hellhammer, D. H., Hubert, W. and Schurmeyer, T. (1985) 'Changes in saliva testosterone after psychological stimulation in men', *Psychoneuroendocrinology*, 10: 77–81.

Hennessey, A. C., Camak, L., Gordon, F. and Edwards, D. A. (1990) 'Connections between the pontine central grey and the ventromedial hypothalamus are essential for lordosis in female rats', *Behavioral Neuroscience*, 104: 477–88.

Hetherington, M. H. and Rolls, B. J. (1996) 'Sensory-specific satiety: theoretical frameworks and central characteristics', in E. D. Capaldi (ed.) *Why We Eat What We Eat*, Washington, DC: American Psychological Association.

Horne, J. A. (1981) 'The effects of exercise on sleep', *Biological Psychology*, 12: 241–91.

—— (1988) *Why We Sleep: The Functions of Sleep in Humans and Other Mammals*, Oxford: Oxford University Press.

Horne, J. A. and Harley, L. J. (1989) 'Human SWS following selective head heating during wakefulness', in J. Horne (ed.) *Sleep '88*, New York: Fischer Verlag.

Huebner, H. F. (1993) *Endorphins, Eating Disorders and Other Addictive Behaviors*, New York: W. W. Norton.

Hull, C. L. (1943) *Principles of Behavior*, New York: Appleton-Century-Crofts.

Hyde, J. S. (1986) 'Gender differences in aggression', in J. S. Hyde and M. C. Linn (eds), *The Psychology of Gender*, Baltimore, MD: Johns Hopkins University Press.

Kevanau, J. L. (1997) 'Origin and evolution of sleep: roles of vision and endothermy', *Brain Research Bulletin*, 42: 245–64.

Kirchgessner, A. L. and Sclafani, A. (1988) 'PVN-hindbrain pathway involved in the hypothalamic hyperphagia-obesity syndrome', *Physiology and Behavior*, 42: 517–28.

Kleitman, N. (1961) 'The nature of dreaming', in G. E. W. Wolstenholme and M. O'Connor (eds), *The Nature of Sleep*, London: J. and A. Churchill.

—— (1982) 'Basic rest–activity cycle – 22 years later', *Sleep*, 4: 311–17.

Koob, G. F. and Bloom, F. E. (1988) 'Cellular and molecular mechanisms of drug dependence', *Science*, 242: 715–23.

Langevin, R., Ben-Aron, M. H., Coulthard, R., Heasman, G., Purins, J. E., Handy, L., Hucker, S. J., Russon, A. E., Day, D., Roper, V., Bain, J., Wortzman, G. and Webster, C. D. (1985) 'Sexual aggression: constructing a predictive equation: a controlled pilot study', in R. Langevin (ed.) *Erotic Preference, Gender Identity and Aggression in Men: New Research Studies*, Hillsdale, NJ: Erlbaum.

Lee, C., Parikh, V., Itsukaichi, T., Bae, K. and Edery, I. (1996) 'Resetting the *Drosophila* clock by photic regulation of PER and a PER-TIM complex', *Science*, 271: 1740–44.

Le Magnen, J. (1990) 'A role for opiates in food reward and food addiction', in E. D. Capaldi and T. L. Powley (eds) *Taste, Experience and Feeding*, Washington, DC: American Psychological Association.

Lesieur, H. R., Bloom, S. B. and Zoppa, R. M. (1986) 'Alcoholism, drug abuse, and gambling', *Alcoholism: Clinical and Experimental Research*, 10: 33–8.

LeVay, S. (1991) 'A difference in hypothalamic structure between heterosexual and homosexual men', *Science*, 253: 1034–7.

Lind, R. W. and Johnson, A. K. (1982) 'Central and peripheral mechanisms mediating angiotensin-induced thirst', in D. Ganten, M. Printz and B. A. Schölkens (eds) *The Renin Angiotensin System in the Brain*, Berlin: Springer-Verlag.

Linden, R. D., Pope, H. G. and Jonas, J. M. (1986) 'Pathological gambling and major affective disorder: preliminary findings', *Journal of Clinical Psychiatry*, 47: 201–3.

Lutz, T. A., Senn, M., Althaus, J., del Prete, E., Ehrensperger, F. and Scharrer, E. (1998) 'Lesion of the area postrema/nucleus of the solitary tract (AP/NTS) attenuates the anorectic effects of amylin and calcitonin gene-related peptide (CGRP) in rats', *Peptides*, 19: 309–17.

McClelland, D. C., Atkinson, J. W., Clark, R. W. and Lowell, E. L. (1953) *The Achievement Motive*, New York: Appleton-Century-Crofts.

McDougall, W. (1908) *Introduction to Social Psychology*, London: Methuen.

McKinney, T. D. and Desjardins, C. (1973) 'Postnatal development of the testis, fighting behavior, and fertility in house mice', *Biology of Reproduction*, 9: 279–94.

McKnight, J. (1997) *Straight Science? Homosexuality, Evolution and Adaptation*, London: Routledge.

McNeill, E. T. (1994) 'Blood, sex and hormones: a theoretical review of women's sexuality over the menstrual cycle', in P. Y. L. Choi and P. Nicholson (eds) *Female Sexuality: Psychology, Biology and Social Context*, Hemel Hempstead: Harvester.

Malsbury, C. W. (1972) 'Facilitation of male rat copulatory behavior by electrical stimulation of the medial preoptic area', *Physiology and Behavior*, 7: 797–805.

Mann, M. A., Konen, C. and Svare, B. (1984) 'The role of progesterone in pregnancy-induced aggression in mice', *Hormones and Behavior*, 18: 140–60.

Mark, V. H. and Ervin, F. R. (1970) *Violence and the Brain*, New York: Harper and Row.

Marshall, E. (1995) 'NIH's "Gay Gene" study questioned', *Science*, 268: 1841.

Marx, R. D. (1994) 'Anorexia nervosa: theories of etiology', in L. Alexander-Mott and D. B. Lumsden (eds), *Understanding Eating Disorders: Anorexia Nervosa, Bulimia Nervosa, and Obesity*, Philadelphia, PA: Taylor and Francis.

Mas, M. (1995) 'Neurobiological correlates of masculine sexual behavior', *Neuroscience and Biobehavioral Reviews*, 19: 261–77.

Maslow, A. H. (1954) *Motivation and Personality*, New York: Harper.

Mayer, J. (1953) 'Glucostatic mechanisms of regulation of food intake', *New England Journal of Medicine*, 249: 13–16.

Mazur, A. and Lamb, T. (1980) 'Testosterone, status, and mood in human males', *Hormones and Behavior*, 14: 236–46.

Mennella, J. A. and Beauchamp, G. K. (1996) 'The early development of human flavor preferences', in E. D. Capaldi (ed.) *Why We Eat What We Eat*, Washington, DC: American Psychological Association.

Meyer-Bahlburg, H. F. L. (1984) 'Psychoendocrine research on sexual orientation: Current status and future options', *Progress in Brain Research*, 63: 375–98.

Mishima, K., Satoh, K., Shimizu, T. and Hishikawa, Y. (1997) 'Hypnotic and hypothermic action of daytime-administered melatonin', *Psychopharmacology*, 133: 168–71.

Money, J. and Ehrhardt, A. (1972) *Man and Woman, Boy and Girl*, Baltimore, MD: Johns Hopkins University Press.

Moore, R. Y. (1983) 'Organization and function of a central nervous system circadian oscillator: the suprachiasmatic nucleus', *Federation Proceedings*, 42: 2783–9.

Moore, R. Y. and Eichler, V. B. (1972) 'Loss of a circadian adrenal corticosterone rhythm following suprachiasmatic lesions in the rat', *Brain Research*, 42: 201–6.

Moore-Ede, M. C. (1982) *The Clocks that Time Us: Physiology of the Circadian Timing System*, Cambridge, MA: Harvard University Press.

Morris, G. O., Williams, H. L. and Lubin, A. (1960) 'Misperception and disorientation during sleep deprivation', *Archives of General Psychiatry*, 2: 247–54.

Moruzzi, G. and Magoun, H. W. (1949) 'Brain stem reticular formation and activation of the EEG', *Electroencephalography and Clinical Neurophysiology*, 1: 455–73.

Motohashi, Y. (1992) 'Alteration of circadian rhythm in shift-working ambulance personnel: Monitoring of salivary cortisol rhythm', *Ergonomics*, 35: 1331–40.

Noonan, M., Smith, M. A., Kelleher, K. and Sanfilippo, M. A. (1998) 'Sex differences in anterior commisure size in the rat', *Brain Research Bulletin*, 45: 101–4.

Nowak, M. A. and Sigmund, K. (1998) 'Evolution of indirect reciprocity by image scoring', *Nature*, 393: 573–7.

Olds, J. and Milner, O. (1954) 'Positive reinforcement produced by electrical stimulation of septal area and other regions of the rat brain', *Journal of Comparative and Physiological Psychology*, 47: 419–27.

Panksepp, J. and Trowill, J. A. (1967) 'Intraoral self-injection: II. The simulation of self-stimulation phenomena with a conventional reward', *Psychonomic Science*, 9: 407–8.

Parmelee, A. H., Schulte, F. J., Akiyama, Y., Wenner, W. H., Schultz, M. A. and Stern, E. (1968) 'Maturation of EEG activity during sleep in premature infants', *Electroencephalography and Clinical Neurophysiology*, 24: 319–29.

Peck, J. W. and Blass, E. M. (1975) 'Localization of thirst and anti-diuretic osmoreceptors by intracranial injections in rats', *American Journal of Physiology*, 5: 1501–9.

Pedrazzi, P., Cattaneo, L., Valeriani, L., Boschi, S., Cocchi, D. and Zoli, M. (1998) 'Hypothalamic neuropeptide Y and galanin in over-weight rats fed a cafeteria diet', *Peptides*, 19: 157–65.

Pfaff, D. W. and Sakuma, Y. (1979) 'Deficit in the lordosis reflex of female rats caused by lesions in the ventromedial nucleus of the hypothalamus', *Journal of Physiology*, 288: 203–10.

Phillips, P. A., Rolls, B. J., Ledingham, J. G. G. and Morton, J. J. (1984) 'Body fluid changes, thirst and drinking in man during free access to water', *Physiology and Behavior*, 33: 357–63.

Phoenix, C. H., Goy, R. W., Gerall, A. A. and Young, W. C. (1959) 'Organizing action of prenatally administered testosterone propi-onate on the tissues mediating mating behavior in the female guinea pig', *Endocrinology*, 65: 369–82.

Pickens, R. and Fletcher, B. (1991) 'Overview of treatment issues', in R. Pickens, C. Leukefeld and C. Schuster (eds) *Improving Drug Abuse Treatment*, Rockville, MD: National Institute on Drug Abuse.

Pilcher, J. J. and Huffcutt, A. J. (1996) 'Effects of sleep deprivation on performance: a meta-analysis', *Sleep*, 19: 318–26.

Pinel, J. P. J., Mana, M. J. and Kim, C. K. (1989) 'Effect-dependent toler-ance to ethanol's anticonvulsant effect on kindled seizures', in R. J. Porter, R. H. Mattson, J. A. Cramer and I. Diamond (eds) *Alcohol and Seizures: Basic Mechanisms and Clinical Implications*, Philadelphia, PA: F. A. Davis.

Ramsay, D. J., Rolls, B. J. and Wood, R. J. (1977) 'Thirst following water deprivation in dogs', *American Journal of Physiology*, 232: R93–100.

Rand, C. S. W. (1994) 'Obesity: definition, diagnostic criteria, and asso-ciated health problems', in L. Alexander-Mott and D. B. Lumsden (eds), *Understanding Eating Disorders: Anorexia Nervosa, Bulimia Nervosa, and Obesity*, Philadelphia, PA: Taylor and Francis.

Rechtschaffen, A., Gilliland, M. A., Bergmann, B. M. and Winter, J. B. (1983) 'Physiological correlates of prolonged sleep deprivation in rats', *Science*, 221: 182–4.

Reinisch, J. M. (1981) 'Prenatal exposure to synthetic progestins increases potential for aggression in humans', *Science*, 211: 561–2.

Rhees, R. W., Shryne, J. E. and Gorski, R. A. (1990) 'Termination of the hormone-sensitive period for differentiation of the sexually dimorphic nucleus of the preoptic area in male and female rats', *Developmental Brain Research*, 52: 17–23.

Ridley, Mark (1996) *Evolution*, second edition, Cambridge, MA: Blackwell.

Ridley, Matt (1996) *The Origins of Virtue*, Harmondsworth: Penguin Books.

Roffwarg, H. P., Muzio, J. N. and Dement, W. C. (1966) 'Ontogenetic development of the human sleep–dream cycle', *Science*, 152: 604–19.

Rolls, E. T. (1993) 'The neural control of feeding in primates', in D. A. Booth (ed.) *Neurophysiology of Ingestion*, Elmsford, NY: Pergamon Press.

Rosenthal, R. J. and Lesieur, H. R. (1992) 'Self-reported withdrawal symptoms and pathological gambling', *American Journal of Addiction*, 1: 150–4.

Russell, M. J., Switz, G. M. and Thompson, K. (1980) 'Olfactory influences on the human menstrual cycle', *Pharmacology, Biochemistry, and Behavior*, 13: 737–8.

Sakai, K. and Jouvet, M. (1980) 'Brain stem PGO-on cells projecting directly to the cat dorsal lateral geniculate nucleus', *Brain Research*, 194: 500–5.

Salamone, J. D., Cousins, M. S. and Snyder, B. J. (1997) 'Behavioral functions of nucleus accumbens dopamine: empirical and conceptual problems with the anhedonia hypothesis', *Neuroscience and Biobehavioral Reviews*, 21: 341–59.

Schaal, B., Tremblay, R. E., Soussignan, R. and Susman, E. J. (1996) 'Male testosterone linked to high social dominance but low physical aggression in early adolescence', *Journal of the American Academy of Child and Adolescent Psychiatry*, 35: 1322–30.

Schafe, G. E. and Bernstein, I. L. (1996) 'Taste aversion learning', in E. D. Capaldi (ed.) *Why We Eat What We Eat*, Washington, DC: American Psychological Association, pp. 31–51.

Schlenker, B. R. (1980) *Impression Management: The Self-Concept, Social Identity, and Interpersonal Relations*, Monterey, CA: Brooks-Cole.

REFERENCES

Schwartz, W. J. and Gainer, H. (1977) 'Suprachiasmatic nucleus: Use of ^{14}C-labelled deoxyglucose uptake as a functional marker', *Science*, 197: 1089–91.

Sclafani, A. and Nissenbaum, J. W. (1988) 'Robust conditioned flavor preference produced by intragastric starch infusion in rats', *American Journal of Physiology*, 255: R672–5.

Sclafani, A., Springer, D. and Kluge, L. (1976) 'Effects of quinine adulteration on the food intake and body weight of obese and nonobese hypothalamic hyperphagic rats', *Physiology and Behavior*, 16: 631–40.

Seta, J. J., Wang, M. A., Crisson, J. E. and Seta, C. E. (1989) 'Audience composition and felt anxiety: impact averaging and summation', *Basic and Applied Social Psychology*, 10: 57–72.

Sforza, E., Montagna, P., Tinuper, P., Cortelli, P., Avoni, P., Ferrillo, F., Petersen, R., Gambetti, P. and Lagaresi, E. (1995) 'Sleep–wake cycle abnormalities in fatal familial insomnia: Evidence of the role of the thalamus in sleep regulation', *Electroencephalography and Clinical Neurophysiology*, 94: 398–405.

Sherwin, B. B. and Gelfand, M. M. (1987) 'The role of androgen in the maintenance of sexual functioning in oopherectomized women', *Psychosomatic Medicine*, 49: 397–409.

Shouse, M. N. and Siegel, J. M. (1992) 'Pontine regulation of REM sleep components in cats: Integrity of the pedunculopontine tegmentum (PPT) is important for phasic events but unnecessary for atonia during REM sleep', *Brain Research*, 571: 50–63.

Siegel, A., Schubert, K. L. and Shaikh, L. (1997) 'Neurotransmitters regulating defensive rage behavior in the cat', *Neuroscience and Biobehavioral Reviews*, 21: 733–42.

Siegel, J. M. (1989) 'Brainstem mechanisms generating REM sleep', in M. H. Kryger, T. Roth and W. C. Dement (eds) *Principles and Practice of Sleep Medicine*, Philadelphia: W. B. Saunders.

Siegel, S. (1978) 'A Pavlovian conditioning analysis of morphine tolerance', in N. A. Krasnegor (ed.) *Behavioral Tolerance: Research and Treatment Implications*, Washington, DC: NIDA Research Monographs.

Siegel, S., Hinson, R. E., Krank, M. D. and McCully, J. (1982) 'Heroin "overdose" death: contribution of drug-associated environmental cues', *Science*, 216: 436–7.

Simpson, J. B., Epstein, A. N. and Camardo, J. S. (1978) 'The localization of dipsogenic receptors for angiotensin II in the subfornical organ', *Journal of Comparative and Physiological Psychology*, 92: 581–608.

Sims, E. A. H. and Horton, E. S. (1968) 'Endocrine metabolic adaptation to obesity and starvation', *American Journal of Clinical Nutrition*, 21: 1455–70.

Smith, C. (1985) 'Sleep states and learning: A review of the animal literature', *Neuroscience and Biobehavioral Reviews*, 9: 157–68.

—— (1995) 'Sleep states and memory processes', *Behavioral Brain Research*, 69: 137–45.

Smith, E., North, C. and Spitznagel, E. (1993) 'Alcohol, drugs, and psychiatric comorbidity among homeless women: an epidemiologic study', *Journal of Clinical Psychiatry*, 54: 82–7.

Smith, G. P. and Gibbs, J. (1994) 'Satiating effect of cholecystokinin', *Annals of the New York Academy of Sciences*, 713: 236–41.

Solomon, P., Kubzansky, P. E., Leiderman, P. H., Mendelson, J. H., Trumbull, R. and Wexler, D. (1961) *Sensory Deprivation*, Cambridge, MA: Harvard University Press.

Squier, M. V., Jalloh, S., Hilton-Jones, D. and Series, H. (1995) 'Death after ecstasy ingestion: neuropathological findings', *Journal of Neurology, Neurosurgery and Psychiatry*, 58: 756.

Stephan, F. K. and Zucker, I. (1972) 'Circadian rhythms in drinking behavior and locomotor activity of rats are eliminated by hypothalamic lesions', in *Proceedings of the National Academy of Sciences, USA*, 69: 1583–6.

Sterman, M. B. and Clemente, C. D. (1962) 'Forebrain inhibitory mechanisms: Sleep patterns induced by basal forebrain stimulation in the behaving cat', *Experimental Neurology*, 6: 103–17.

Stern, K. and McClintock, M. K. (1998) 'Regulation of ovulation by human pheromones', *Nature*, 392: 177–9.

Stewart, D. A. and Brown, S. A. (1995) 'Withdrawal and dependency symptoms among adolescent alcohol and drug users', *Addiction*, 90: 627–35.

Stunkard, A. J., Sørenson, T. I. A., Harris, C., Teasdale, T. W., Chakraborty, R., Schull, W. J. and Schulsinger, F. (1986) 'An adoption study of human obesity', *New England Journal of Medicine*, 314: 193–8.

Svare, B. (1989) 'Recent advances in the study of female aggressive behavior in mice', in S. Parmigiani, D. Mainardi and P. Brain (eds) *House Mouse Aggression: A Model for Understanding the Evolution of Social Behavior*, London: Gordon and Breach.

REFERENCES

Swaab, D. F. and Hofman, M. A. (1990) 'An enlarged suprachiasmatic nucleus in homosexual men', *Brain Research*, 537: 141–8.

Swaab, D. F., Slob, A. K., Houtsmuller, E. J. and Brand, T. (1995) 'Increased number of vasopressin neurons in the suprachiasmatic nucleus (SCN) of "bisexual" adult male rats following perinatal treatment with the aromatase blocker ATD', *Developmental Brain Research*, 85: 273–9.

Swithers, S. E. and Hall, W. G. (1994) 'Does oral experience terminate ingestion?', *Appetite*, 23: 113–38.

Szymusiak, R. and McGinty, D. (1989) 'Sleep suppression following kainic acid-induced lesions of the basal forebrain', *Experimental Neurology*, 94: 598–614.

Takahashi, L. K. (1990) 'Hormonal regulation of sociosexual behavior in female mammals', *Neuroscience and Biobehavioral Reviews*, 14: 403–13.

Tanaka, J., Ushigome, A., Hori, K. and Nomura, M. (1998) 'Responses of raphe nucleus projecting subfornical organ neurons to angiotensin II in rats', *Brain Research Bulletin*, 45: 315–18.

Teitelbaum, P. and Stellar, E. (1954) 'Recovery from failure to eat produced by hypothalamic lesions', *Science*, 120: 894–5.

Trivers, R. L. (1971) 'The evolution of reciprocal altruism', *Quarterly Review of Biology*, 46: 35–57.

Vaccarino, F. J., Bloom, R. E. and Koob, G. F. (1985) 'Blockade of nucleus accumbens opiate receptors attenuates intravenous heroin reward in the rat', *Psychopharmacology*, 86: 37–42.

van de Poll, N. E., Taminiau, M. S., Endert, E. and Louwerse, A. L. (1988) 'Gonadal steroid influence upon sexual and aggressive behavior of female rats', *International Journal of Neuroscience*, 41: 271–86.

van Goozen, S. H. M., Frijda, N. H. and van de Poll, N. E. (1995) 'Anger and aggression during role-playing: gender differences between hormonally treated male and female transsexuals and controls', *Aggressive Behavior*, 21: 257–73.

van Goozen, S. H. M., Frijda, N. H., Wiegant, V. M., Endert, E. and van de Poll, N. E. (1996) 'The premenstrual phase and reactions to aversive events: an experimental study on anger and aggression proneness in women', *Psychoneuroendocrinology*, 21: 479–97.

van Goozen, S. H. M., Wiegant, V. M., Endert, E., Helmond, F. A. and van de Poll, N. E. (1997) 'Psychoendocrinological assessment of the menstrual cycle: the relationship between hormones, sexuality, and mood', *Archives of Sexual Behavior*, 26: 359–82.

Verbalis, J. G. (1991) 'Inhibitory controls of drinking: Satiation of thirst', in D. J. Ramsay and D. A. Booth (eds) *Thirst: Physiological and Psychological Aspects*, London: Springer-Verlag.

vom Saal, F. S. (1983) 'Models of early hormone effects on intrasex aggression in mice', in B. B. Svare (ed.) *Hormones and Aggressive Behavior*, New York: Plenum Press.

Wagner, H. L. (1988) 'The theory and application of social psychophysiology', in H. L. Wagner (ed.) *Social Psychophysiology and Emotion*, Chichester: John Wiley.

Wagner, H. L. and Smith, J. (1991) 'Facial expression in the presence of friends and strangers', *Journal of Nonverbal Behavior*, 15: 201–14.

Wallen, K. (1996) 'Nature needs nurture: the interaction of hormonal and social influences on the development of behavioral sex differences in rhesus monkeys', *Hormones and Behavior*, 30: 364–78.

Walsh, R. (1992) 'Sociocultural perspectives on substance abuse disorders', *American Journal of Psychiatry*, 149: 1760–1.

Webb, W. B. (1978) 'The sleep of conjoined twins', *Sleep*, 1: 205–11.

Webster, H. H. and Jones, B. E. (1988) 'Neurotoxic lesions of the dorsolateral pontomesencephalic tegmentum-cholinergic cell area in the cat. II. Effects upon sleep–waking states', *Brain Research*, 458: 285–302.

Weingarten, H. P. (1983) 'Conditioned cues elicit feeding in sated rats: a role for learning in meal initiation', *Science*, 220: 431–2.

Welsh, D. K., Logothetis, D. E., Meister, M. and Reppert, S. M. (1995) 'Individual neurons dissociated from rat suprachiasmatic nucleus express independently phased circadian firing rhythms', *Neuron*, 14: 697–706.

White, N. M. (1996) 'Addictive drugs as reinforcers: multiple partial actions on memory systems', *Addiction*, 91: 921–49.

Wilson, H. C. (1992) 'A critical review of menstrual synchrony research', *Psychoneuroendocrinology*, 17: 565–91.

Wise, R. A. and Bozarth, M. A. (1987) 'A psychomotor stimulant theory of addiction', *Psychological Review*, 94: 469–92.

Wood, R. I. (1997) 'Thinking about networks in the control of male hamster sexual behavior', *Hormones and Behavior*, 32: 40–5.

Woods, S. C. (1995) 'Insulin and the brain: a mutual dependency', *Progress in Psychobiology*, 16: 53–81.

Woods, S. C., Chavez, M., Park, C. R., Riedy, C., Kaiyala, K., Richardson, R. D., Figlewicz, D. P., Schwartz, M. W., Porte, D. and Seeley, R. J. (1996) 'The evaluation of insulin as a metabolic

REFERENCES

signal influencing behavior via the brain', *Neuroscience and Biobehavioral Reviews*, 20: 139–44.

Young, W. G. and Deutsch, J. A. (1980) 'Intragastric pressure and receptive relaxation in the rat', *Physiology and Behavior*, 25: 973–5.

Zajonc, R. B. (1965) 'Social facilitation', *Science*, 149: 269–74.

Zellner, D. A., Rozin, P., Aron, M. and Kulish, D. (1983) 'Conditioned enhancement of humans' liking for flavors paired with sweetness', *Learning and Motivation*, 14: 338–50.

Zhou, J. N., Hofman, M. A. and Swaab, D. F. (1995) 'No changes in the number of vasoactive intestinal polypeptide (VIP)-expressing neurons in the suprachiasmatic nucleus of homosexual men; comparison with vasopressin-expressing neurons', *Brain Research*, 672: 285–8.

Zillmann, D. (1989) 'Aggression and sex: independent and joint operations', in H. Wagner and A. Manstead (eds) *Handbook of Social Psychophysiology*, Chichester: John Wiley.

Zucker, I., Boshes, M. and Dark, J. (1983) 'Suprachiasmatic nuclei influence circannual and circadian rhythms of ground squirrels', *American Journal of Physiology*, 244: R472–80.

Index

Lightning Source UK Ltd.
Milton Keynes UK
UKOW06f0014120816

280505UK00001B/12/P